Douglas

RON MAK

KEY
Books

HISTORIC COMMERCIAL AIRCRAFT SERIES, VOLUME 7

Published by Key Books
An imprint of Key Publishing Ltd
PO Box 100
Stamford
Lincs PE19 1XQ

www.keypublishing.com

All images are from the author's collection, unless
otherwise stated.

The right of Ron Mak to be identified as the
author of this book has been asserted in accordance
with the Copyright, Designs and Patents Act 1988
Sections 77 and 78.

ISBN 978 1 80282 432 2

Typeset by SJmagic DESIGN SERVICES, India.

Introduction

Excluding military variants, sales of the Boeing 707 family of large jet airliners are about double those of their nearest rival: the Douglas DC-8; yet, with nearly 400 of all Douglas DC-8 variants ordered, the DC-8 design is far from being overshadowed by Boeing at Renton. The Douglas DC-8, which began life as the Douglas Model 1881, became available to the airliners about a year after the first Boeing 707s, but, from the outset, Douglas regarded this time lag as an advantage rather than otherwise. In particular, it determined that safety and performance standards should be maintained without loss of flying qualities, and, unlike Boeing, was able to pursue its design unhampered by consideration of military requirements. The decision to proceed with what was then envisaged as a domestic airliner was taken in June 1955, and, in the following October, the first 25 orders came from Pan American World Airways. By the end of 1955, an intercontinental model had also been proposed, and Douglas had received DC-8 orders from three more US airlines (United Air Lines, National Airlines and Eastern Air Lines), two European carriers (KLM and SAS) and one from Japan (Japan Air Lines). By 30 May 1958, when the JT3C-powered prototype N8008D made its first flight, the order book stood at more than a 130 aircraft.

Standard DC-8s have been built in five basic versions: two for domestic routes and three for intercontinental operation. The domestic models are the series DC-8-10, with 13,500lb st JT3C-6 turbojets, and the series DC-8-20, powered by 15,800lb st JT4A-3s. The intercontinental series DC-8-30 offers a choice of JT4A-9 or 11 engines; the series DC-8-40 uses Rolls-Royce Conway 509s 17,500lb st; and series DC-8-50 has JT3D-1 or 3 turbofans. The first DC-8-20 was flown on 29 November 1958, the DC-8-30 and -40 on 21 February and 23 July 1959, respectively, and the first DC-8-50 on 20 December 1960. The DC-8-10 was the first model to go into operation, entering service simultaneously with United Air Lines and Delta on 18 September 1959. Meanwhile, Douglas had introduced drag-reducing modifications to the wing, which involved a new leading edge and wing tip profile with leading edge shots. Thus modified, on 21 August 1961, the DC-8-40 made the first flight at over Mach 1 by a jet airliner when it reached 667mph (1,073km/hr) in a shallow dive, equivalent to Mach 1.012.

Numerically, the most successful variant has been the series -50, and some domestic DC-8s have been converted to this standard. In April 1961, Douglas announced a further variant, the Douglas DC-8F Jet Trader, which was an all-cargo or mixed-traffic version of the series -50, with JT3D-3 fan engines, reinforced floor and increased gross weight. The first Douglas DC-8F was flown on 29 October 1962, and this version was available in basic form as the DC-8-54 and in improved form, with JT3D-3B engines, as the Douglas DC-8-55. Maximum capacity of the Jet Trader was 95,282lb or 189 passengers. Excluding the 'Super Sixty' variants, about 260 DC-8s, of the 300 or so on order, were in airline service at the beginning of 1967.

The Super Sixty Series

Three stretched and improved variants of the Douglas DC-8 were a healthy addition to the Douglas order book. Over 130 examples for this four-jet aircraft had been ordered since the first details were announced in April 1965. Under the generic title 'Super Sixty', these comprised the DC-8-61,

DC-8-62 and DC-8-63, all of which had the same powerplant and could be used in passenger, cargo or mixed-traffic layouts. First in service was the DC-8-61 with United Air Lines from November 1966. It had a fuselage 36ft 8in longer than the standard DC-8-50, seating from 234 to 251 passengers and providing additional baggage/cargo space. Primarily a high-density domestic model, the DC-8-61 was flown for the first time on 14 March 1966 and received its type certification from the Federal Aviation Administration (FAA) on 2 September.

The maiden flight of the DC-8-62 took place on 29 August 1966, and this was a more drastically redesigned version. Although its 189-passenger fuselage was only 6ft 8in longer than the DC-8-50, it had longer, repositioned engine pods and new drag-reducing wing tip extensions, which increased the overall span by 6ft. The internal wing structure was also modified to increase fuel tankage for extra-long ranges. Certification was granted in the spring of 1967, and the first deliveries to SAS took place shortly afterward.

By then, the first flight of the DC-8-63 had occurred. The DC-8-63 combined the long fuselage of the DC-8-61 with the new wings and other aerodynamic refinements of all the many DC-8 variants; at its full take-off weight, it required more runway than any other commercial aircraft at that time in service. Certification of the DC-8-63 occurred in 1968. The first deliveries were PH-DEA and PH-DEB of KLM Royal Dutch Airlines.

As examples of the range/payload potential of the Super Sixty series, the DC-8-61 prototype had flown 5,630 miles (9,060km) non-stop from California to Tokyo, and the DC-8-62 was capable of non-stop flights from the US Pacific seaboard to points in central Europe with a 40,000lb payload. A total of 556 Douglas DC-8s were built. Some DC-8s are still in service, as their airframe life is excellent, and some were re-engined with the CFM56 turbofan, providing fuel-efficient propulsion and a much higher flight performance; the re-engined aircraft will be styled as -70 series.

As of 2022, there are six DC-8s still active in North America and Africa:

- 45990 OB-2059-P Douglas DC-8-73CF, with Skybus Heavylift As of February 2022, it was flying Miami, Florida, to Santo Domingo, Dominican Republic.
- 46013 N782SP Douglas DC-8-72CF, with Samaritan's Purse. This was very active during March and April 2022 flying from Greensboro, North Carolina, to Rzeszow, Poland, near the border of the Ukraine.
- 46082 N817NA Douglas DC-8-72, with NASA. As of January 2022, it was flying Palmdale–Palmdale.
- 46091 OB-2158-P Douglas DC-8-73CF, also with Skybus Heavylift. In April 2022, it was flying from Miami to Managua, Nicaragua.
- 46110 9S-AJG Douglas DC-8-62F, with Trans Air Cargo Service. It has been flying almost daily from Kinshasa N`Djili International Airport to several destinations in the Democratic Republic of the Congo, including Lubumbashi, Goma, Kisangani and Mbuji Mayi.
- 46133 9S-AJO Douglas DC-8-73F, also of Trans Air Cargo Service. In April, it received a C-check at Kinshasa N`Djili International Airport, after which it flew to Johannesburg Tambo International Airport for more maintenance and paperwork.

Ron Mak
April 2022
The Netherlands

Douglas DC-8

N8008D DC-8-11, number one off the production line, made its first flight on 30 May 1958; it was airborne for 2 hours, 7 minutes. It was used for flight testing before being converted to a DC-8-51 and leased to National Airlines from 21 June 1961 until 26 May 1962. It was then bought by Trans International and leased to Lufthansa from May 1965 until December 1965. Its next lease was with Canadian Pacific as CF-CPN and then Aeroméxico as XA-DOE. It was bought by F A Ayer and stored at Marana in Arizona as N8008D. It was finally sold to Agro Air in May 1989 for spare parts and broken up in 2001. (Geoffrey Thomas Collection)

N800PA Douglas DC-8-32/33 Pan American World Airways *Flying Cloud*. Pan American changed its original order for the Douglas DC-8 jets so that it took delivery of only 19 of the 25 DC-8s ordered. It went on to buy many Boeing 707s, such was the relationship struck up between Pan American and Boeing. N800PA DC-8-32/33 Pan American, from the Douglas plant in Long Beach, was delivered on 2 June 1961. It was bought by Panair do Brasil on 26 September 1962 as PP-PEA, after almost three years of service, and then sold to Varig in June 1965. On 4 March 1967, during a flight from Rome to Monrovia in Liberia, it crashed on the approach to Monrovia Airport. (Geoffrey Thomas Collection)

N802PA DC-8-32/33 was delivered to Pan American World Airways on 15 February 1961 as *Clipper Cathay.* **It was bought by Delta Air Lines as N8027 in August 1969. Sold to Charlotte Aircraft Corporation on 23 January 1974, it was leased to Trabajos y Fe Transportes Aéreos (TRAFE) from Argentina as LV-LTP. It was withdrawn from use and stored at Buenos Aires Ezeiza Airport in May 1980. The aircraft was destroyed in a fire on 13 December 1992.**

N809PA Douglas DC-8-32/33, *Clipper Great Republic,* **Pan American World Airways at New York Idlewild Airport, 15 February 1961. In the background you can see N802PA and N806PA – both Pan American World Airways aircraft. It was delivered on 22 June 1960 as N809PA and sold afther eight years of service to United Airlines as N8246U on 18 October 1968. It subsequently passed through a number of airlines and lease companies: Overseas National Airways, Aire Cardinal International, United Air Leasing – converted to a freighter in 1977 – Rosenbalm Aviation, Emery World and International Airline Support, which bought the DC-8-33(F) on 29 December 1984. It was stored and broken up at Miami Airport in January 1986. (Bob Parrick)**

OO-TCP Douglas DC-8-32/33 Pomair at Ostend Airport, 9 September 1973. It was originally delivered to Pan American World Airways on 10 September 1960 as N812PA, then bought by Pomair on May 1971 and leased to Air France and Air Ceylon during 1973–74. It was sold to Capitol International Airways on May 1975 and leased to Trabajos Aéreos Enlaces (TAE) as EC-CUS. It returned to Capitol in February 1977 and was sold to United Air Leasing in August 1978. It was leased to Saudi Arabian Airlines as N900CL in July 1979 before returning to United Air Leasing. Bought by Rosenbalm Aviation in January 1982, it was stored and withdrawn from use at Medford Airport in Oregon. It was broken up in June 1982.

N8148A Douglas DC-8-33F Intercontinental Airways, Miami Airport in October 1977. It was was originally delivered to Pan American Airways as N814PA in October 1960 and then bought by Delta Air Lines on 30 December 1968 as N8148A. It was sold to Charlotte Aircraft Corporation on January 1974 and converted to a Douglas DC-8-33F on March 1974. Intercontinental Airways leased the aircraft in October 1977, buying it in October 1978. It was leased to Ecuatoriana and Aerocondor Colombia from July 1979 until June 1980 and then returned to Intercontinental before being sold to Charlotte Aircraft Corporation in October 1981. It was stored at Laurinburg-Maxton Airport, New Carolina, in September 2004 and broken up .

9Q-CLF Douglas DC-8-32/33 Air Congo at Hellinikon Airport, Athens, 8 April 1973. Originally delivered to Pan American World Airways as N815PA *Clipper Charger* in November 1960, it was leased to Air Congo in December 1968 and bought in June 1969 as 9Q-CLF. The airline's name changed to Air Zaïre in October 1971. The DC-8 was stored at Kinshasa in November 1974, where it was broken up. Air Congo was formed on 28 June 1961 as the national airline of the Congo and operations began from Kinshasa with a Boeing 707 leased from Sabena; the first DC-8 arrived in 1968.

N8166A Douglas DC-8-33F Rich International Airways at Miami Airport, 1 November 1979. Originally delivered to Pan American World Airways as N816PA on 10 November 1960, *Clipper East Indian* was sold to Delta Air Lines as N8166A in December 1968. It was bought by Charlotte Aircraft Corporation in January 1974 and converted to a Douglas DC-8-33F. It was sold to Intercontinental Airways in October 1977, bought by Rich International Airways in August 1979, and sold again, this time to JAERO, in September. It was then leased to Faucett and Angola Airlines, returned to JAERO and bought by Linhas Aéreas de São Tomé e Principe in November 1987. It was withdrawn from use and stored at Luanda Airport in Angola. It was broken up in May 1988.

PP-PDS Douglas DC-8-33 Varig at Rio de Janeiro Galeao Airport, July 1973. Ordered by Pan American World Airways as N819PA Douglas DC-8-33, it was not taken up. The order went to Panair do Brasil, delivered on 21 March 1961 as PP-PDS. It was sold to Varig in June 1965 and stored at Porto Alegre Airport from 1969 until October 1975. American Jet Industries bought it in February 1978 as N59AJ, converted it to a DC-8-33(F), and it was stored at Mojave Airport in California in 1985. It was exported to Panama as HP-1166TCA in September 1991 for Tocumen Air Cargo and sub-leased to Aeronaves del Perú. It was also leased to Export Air as OB-1456. It was damaged beyond repair at Iquitos Airport in Perú on 28 March 1992. (Michel Anciaux)

N220RB Douglas DC-8-21 Project Orbis at Amsterdam Airport Schiphol, 6 July 1988. It was delivered to United Air Lines on 16 June 1960 as N8003U and converted from a DC-8-11 to a DC-8-21 in May 1965. It was donated to Project Orbis, Inc. on 12 March 1980, re-registered as N220RB in January 1982, and used as a Flying Eye Hospital: Orbis operates hospital-based programmes in several countries and works with local medical research and healthcare organisations on blindness prevention and eye disease treatment. In April 1994, it was donated the Datangshan Museum in Beijing, China.

XA-LSA Douglas DC-8-21F Aero León S A at Tocumen Airport, Panama City, 13 November 1980. Delivered to United Air Lines as N8027U on 25 May 1960, *Mainliner Kauai* was bought by Sun Land Airlines in November 1978 and sold to United Air Leasing in March 1979. It was converted to a Douglas DC-8-21(F) on June 1979 and bought by Southern Air Transport on July 1979 before being leased to Aero León S A as XA-LSA from July 1979 until January 1984. The aircraft's registration was changed to N4929U, and it was stored at Miami Airport. It was broken up in 1986.

N99862 Douglas DC-8-52 Cyprus Airways at Amsterdam Airport Schiphol, 8 April 1977. Delivered to United Air Lines on 8 June 1961 as N8036U, it was leased to Air New Zealand from November 1970 until June 1971, after which it was bought as ZK-NZF and then sold to Douglas as N99862 in March 1976. It was leased to Cyprus Airways from 30 March 1976 until March 1978 as N99862, returned to Douglas, bought by Evergreen International as N804EV and leased to Libyan Arab Airlines. It was finally returned to Evergreen International and stored at Marana Airport in Arizona in November 1979. It was broken up in January 1984.

PH-DCA Douglas DC-8-32/33 KLM Royal Dutch Airlines *Albert Plesman* (delivered on 19 March 1960) at Amsterdam Airport Schiphol, May 1960. Bought by Belgian International Air Service (BIAS) on 17 April 1972 as OO-AMI, it was sold to Delta International in January 1973 and then bought by Pomair in May 1973. It was sold to Luchtvaart Investerings Maatschappij as PH-DCA in October 1974 and leased to Martinair and Garuda Indonesian Airways. The aircraft was bought by Capitol International Airways in December 1975 as N904CL and then leased to Saudia and Air Fleets International. It was returned to Overseas National Airways in November 1980 and broken up at Fort Lauderdale in May 1981. (KLM Aerocarto)

PH-DCA Douglas DC-8-32/33 BIAS at Amsterdam Airport Schiphol, 13 April 1972. BIAS was a Belgian airline with its headquarters in Antwerp and Brussels. Operational between 1959 and 1980, it offered mainly passenger and cargo air charter flights from Brussels Airport to the former Belgian colonies in Central Africa, operating the following aircraft: de Havilland Dove, Heron, Douglas DC3, DC4, DC6, DC8, Fokker F27 and F28 and Sud Aviation Caravelle. This ex-KLM DC-8-32/33 was the airline's first big jet besides the Caravelle.

PH-DCB Douglas DC-8-32/33 Venezolana International de Aviación S A (VIASA)/KLM at Amsterdam Airport Schiphol, 18 September 1972. It was delivered to KLM on 18 April 1960 and leased as *Bali*, in full colours with a Dutch registration, to Garuda Indonesian Airways from March 1969 until February 1972. After returning to KLM, it was bought by VIASA on 27 September 1972 as YV-C-VIE and re-registered as YV-127C in June 1975. Sold to United Aircraft Leasing in December 1975 as N53CA, it was converted to a DC-8-33(F) and bought by Conner Air Lines, then leased to Airlift International, and returned to Conner before being withdrawn from use at Miami Airport. It was broken up in 1996.

PH-DCC Douglas DC-8-32/33 KLM Royal Dutch Airlines at Amsterdam Airport Schiphol, 29 May 1970. The aircraft was delivered on 9 May 1960. *Sir Frank Whittle* was leased to Philippine Airlines (PAL) on 3 April 1970 as PI-C827 (PI stands for Philippine Islands). It was re-registered as RP-C827 in January 1974 (RP stands for Philippine Republic.) It was sold to FB Ayer & Associates, Inc. in May 1978 as N833FA. The airline became FBA Corporation in April 1982, and the aircraft was stored at Opa Locka Airport, Florida, and broken up in June 1983.

PH-DCD Douglas DC-8-32/33 Martinair Holland at Amsterdam Airport Schiphol, 27 September 1973. It was first delivered to KLM Royal Dutch Airlines on 4 July 1960, then bought by Martinair Holland in November 1967 and leased to KLM on 15 November 1967. It was then bought by KLM on 28 March 1970 and leased to Martinair Holland on 1 February 1972. The aircraft was sold to African Safari Airways on 1 November 1973 as 5Y-ASA and bought by Transmeridian Air Cargo in May 1977 as G-BETJ. It was used for spare parts, stored at London Stansted Airport and broken up in July 1985.

5Y-ASA Douglas DC-8-32/33 African Safari Airways at Amsterdam Airport Schiphol, 28 October 1976. African Safari Airways was an airline based in Mombasa, Kenya. It operated charter flights and inclusive tours from 1967, later offering Bristol Britannia flights from mainly European airports such as London Gatwick, Frankfurt, Munich, Basel, Milan, Rome, Vienna and Paris from 1969 until 1972. The DC-8-32/33 flights started in December 1973, with a DC-8-53 introduced in 1976 and a DC-8-63 in 1982.

PH-DCF Douglas DC-8-32/33 Garuda Indonesian Airways/KLM Royal Dutch Airlines at Amsterdam Airport Schiphol, 5 April 1969. Delivered to KLM Royal Dutch Airlines on 24 September 1960, *Anthony Fokker* was leased to Martinair Holland from June 1967 until June 1968. It was then returned to KLM and leased to Garuda Indonesian Airways as *Java* from 1 October 1969 until 25 February 1972. After returning to KLM, it was bought by VIASA on 8 March 1973 as YV-C-VIF and later re-registered as YV-128C in October 1975. It was sold to United Air Leasing on 18 October 1977 as N71UA and bought by Zantop International Airlines in March 1978. The aircarft was broken up at Willow Run Airport, Detroit, in July 1978.

PH-DCG Douglas DC-8-32/33 KLM Royal Dutch Airlines at Manila Airport, August 1968. Ordered by KLM and delivered on 26 October 1960, it was bought by BIAS as OO-CMB on 7 March 1972, sold to Delta International on February 1973 and bought by Pomair in May 1973. A Dutch investment company bought the DC-8 in October 1974 as PH-DCG, and it was leased to Martinair Holland and Garuda from December 1974 until April 1975. The aircraft was then sold to Capitol International Airways as N903CL in May 1975, leased to ALM Antillean Airlines, sold to Overseas National Airways (ONA) in May 1979, and bought by United African Airlines as 5A-DGN on 3 March 1980. It was stored at Luxemburg Airport and broken up in October 1981.

HS-TGO Douglas DC-8-32/33 Thai International at Hong Kong Kai Tak Airport, 27 March 1972. It was delivered to SAS as SE-DBA on 11 May 1960, bought by International Airlease in April 1970 and leased to Thai International from April 1970 until March 1978. It was then sold to United Air Leasing as N715UA and converted to a DC-8-33(F) before being sold to Tropical Aircraft Leasing (TAL). Leased to Polair, Inc. in April 1979 until December 1979, it returned to TAL and was leased again to Aeronaves del Perú in August 1980. On 12 September 1980, the aircraft crashed on its approach to Iquitos Airport in Perú and was damaged beyond repair.

N804E Douglas DC-8-51 Mackey International Airlines at Amsterdam Airport Schiphol, 22 September 1980. This aircraft began its life with Delta Air Lines on October 1959 and served with the carrier until June 1979. It was bought by FB Ayer in July 1979 and was converted from a DC-8-11/12 to a DC-8-51 before being leased to Mackey from September 1979 until September 1980. It was then leased to Airlift International and returned to FB Ayer in June 1981. Stored at Marana Airport in Arizona, the aircraft was broken up in March 1993.

LX-IDB Douglas DC-8-53 Bangladesh Biman at Amsterdam Airport Schiphol, 30 November 1980. Originally delivered to Swissair as HB-IDB on 19 June 1960, the DC-8-32/33 was converted to a series 53 in February 1964. It was sold to TAG Aeronautics in March 1976 and leased to Cargo Lux, Air Algerie and Pakistan International Airlines during October 1978 and April 1980. After being leased to Bangladesh Biman from November 1980 until May 1981, it was sold to United African Airlines in August 1981 as 5A-DGL and re-registered as 5A-DJD in November 1981. The aircraft was sold to Excelair in June 1983 as N3951B. Stored at Brussels Airport, it was withdrawn from use and broken up during August 1984. (Peter de Groot)

S9-NAB Douglas DC-8-33(F) Transafrik at Johannesburg Airport, 6 September 1988. Delivered to Japan Air Lines as JA8005 on 23 November 1960, it was bought by American Jet Industries in May 1974 as N421AJ and leased by several airlines like Rosenbalm Aviation, Zantop International Airlines and Emery Worldwide before being bought by International Airline Support Group in December 1984. The airline was renamed International Air Tours and the aircraft re-registered as 5N-AYZ. It was sold to Transafrik in January 1987 as S9-NAB and stored and broken up at Johannesburg Airport in October 1989. (Andy Heap)

EC-CDA Douglas DC-8-21 Air Spain at Amsterdam Airport Schiphol, 28 July 1973. Air Spain was a Spanish charter airline that operated from 1965 to 1975, declaring bankruptcy in 1975. With its main base at Palma de Mallorca, it started operations in May 1967 using Bristol Brittania aircraft, which were replaced by Douglas DC-8s. N8608 was delivered to Eastern Air Lines on 8 August 1960 and bought by Air Spain on 11 April 1973. It was sold to Hamarein Air in February 1977 as A6-SHA and leased to Bursa Hava Yollari as TC-JBV on 4 March 1980. The aircraft was broken up at Beek Airport, Maastricht, in December 1984.

N819F Douglas DC-8-21 Pakistan International Airlines (PIA) at Amsterdam Airport Schiphol, 24 April 1978. Originally ordered by Eastern Air Lines as N8617 in October 1961, it was bought by ONA on 26 September 1973 and sold to United Air Leasing, which leased the aircraft to several airlines including PIA. It was then converted to a DC-8- 21(F) model and leased to Zantop International Airlines, Rosenbalm, Swiftair Cargo, Emery Worldwide Airlines and finally sold to the International Airline Support Group in December 1984. It as broken up at Miami Airport, Florida, during 1986.

EC-CDC Douglas DC-8-32/33 TAE at Düsseldorf Airport, 3 October 1980. TAE was an airline based in Spain that operated from 1967 until 1981. It acquired three Douglas DC-7s and later one BAC 1-11, three Caravelles and five DC-8s, ceasing operations in November 1981. N9601Z was first flown on 24 March 1960 for Douglas and sold to Union Aeromaritime de Transport (UAT) as F-BJLA, delivered on 27 June 1960. UAT merged with Union de Transports Aériens (UTA) in October 1963. The aircraft was bought by TAE on 6 June 1973; it was withdrawn from use at Palma de Mallorca Airport and broken up in July 1984.

OB-R1143 Douglas DC-8-43(F) AeroPerú Cargo Aeronaves del Perú at Miami Airport, February 1988. It crashed into the fog-shrouded Cerro Lilio mountain range near Mexico City on 1 August 1980. Aeronaves del Perú had many operational DC-8s in its fleet: a total of 12 between 1980 and 1992. Delivered to Alitalia on 28 April 1960, I-DIWA was sold to International Air Leases, Inc. as N64799 on 10 October 1977. It was leased to Saudia and Queen of the World between October 1977 and July 1978, converted to a DC-8-43(F) and leased to Aeronaves del Perú in November 1978.

9J-ABR Douglas DC-8-42/43 Zambia Airways at London Heathrow Airport, 8 August 1970. Zambia Airways was established in 1964 as a subsidiary of Central African Airways. The carrier operated on domestic and international routes for more than 30 years, until it ceased operations in 1995. Starting with two Douglas DC-3s and three de Havilland Beavers in 1964, it received two BAC 1-11s in 1968 and a Douglas DC-8-42/43 was wet-leased from Alitalia in November 1968 to start flights from Lusaka via Nairobi and Rome to London Heathrow. A second DC-8 was added from Alitalia in 1970. IAS Cargo Airlines bought the DC-8 on 1 January 1976. It was broken up in August 1976 at Luton Airport .

I-DIWI Douglas DC-8-42/43 Alitalia at Hellinikon Airport, Athens, 6 April 1973. Delivered to Alitalia on 22 July 1960, it was sold to International Air Leases, Inc. as N64804 on 27 August 1977 and leased to several airlines, such as Saudia, Libyan Arab Airlines and Bahamas World Airlines. It returned to International Air Leases in June 1980 and stored at Miami Airport Florida before being bought by Aeronaves del Perú in May 1981 as OB-R1214. It was converted to a DC-8-43(F) in June 1981, leased to Faucett for several months and stored at Lima Airport in June1986. The aircarft was boken up in December 1988.

N801US, a Douglas DC-8-32, was delivered to Northwest Orient Airlines (NWO) on 18 May 1960. It was operational with NWO until 15 September 1963 when it was sold to National Airlines as N7181C in December 1972. Spear Air from Finland bought the DC-8 on 8 December 1972 with the registration OH-SOB. It was only in service for 20 months before being sold to Overseas National Airways as N1776R on 20 September 1974. It was bought by the United Air Leasing Corp in October 1977 and leased to PIA, seen at Amsterdam Airport Schiphol on 24 April 1978. It was leased to other airlines, including Egyptair, Tunis Air and Saudi, before being stored at Jeddah and broken up in March 1981.

4R-ACQ Douglas DC-8-53 Air Ceylon at Le Bourget Airport, Paris, 12 May 1972. Air Ceylon is the government-owned airline of Sri Lanka, formerly known as Ceylon. Founded in 1947 as Ceylon Airways, operations began on 10 December with a service from Colombo to Madras in India. In the following year, the airlines's name was changed to Air Ceylon, and the network was futher extended to Singapore and London, with two DC-8s in service. Delivered to NWO as N803US on 11 August 1960, this aircaft was bought by UAT as F-BLLC in 1962. It was converted from a DC-8-32 to a 53 in September 1965 and leased by Air Ceylon from April 1972 until October 1978. It was bought by F B Ayer as N53KM and broken up at Miami in 1984.

HC-BEI Douglas DC-8-32(F) Andes Airlines at Miami Airport, 20 November 1980. This all-cargo carrier know as Andes Airlines was established in 1961 by Captain Alfredo Franco. For the first year, various freight charters were undertaken with Douglas DC-3s and Curtiss C-46s, and in 1966 a twice-weekly scheduled cargo and mail service was inaugurated between Guayaquil in Ecuador and Miami via Quito and Panama City. Its first DC-8-32(F) was leased from United Air Leasing in October 1977 and bought on September 1982. The aircraft was broken up at Guayaquil Airport in August 1985.

OH-SOA Douglas DC-8-32 Spear Air at Amsterdam Airport Schiphol, 8 May 1973. Spear Tours was a Finnish travel agency active in the 1960s and '70s, operating flights from Finland to continental Spain and to the Canary Islands, with almost 100,000 passengers per year from 1965 to 1974. The company went bankrupt in 1974, mostly due to increased fuel prices caused by the 1973 oil crisis. It had two DC-8s in service, OH-SOA and OH-SOB, which was an ex-Northwest Orient Airlines aircraft, N805US, delivered on 4 January 1961. It was broken up at Guayaquil Airport in Ecuador as HC-BEI.

PI-C804 Douglas DC-8-53 KLM Royal Dutch Airlines at Amsterdam Airport Schiphol, 17 June 1972. It was delivered to the Douglas Aircraft Company as N9607Z and sold to Philippine Airlines as PI-C801 on 27 February 1962 but directly stored at Las Vegas Airport. KLM leased the aircraft as PH-DCR from 8 August 1962 until 23 December 1967. It was then re-registered as PI-C804 on December 1967 and leased again to KLM as PI-C804 on 1 May 1972. The aircraft was returned to Philippine Airlines on March 1975 as PI-C804 and bought by African Air Charter on 25 October 1983 as 9Q-CQM. In August 1988, it was withdrawn from use and broken up at Kinshasa N'Djili Airport.

9Q-CLV Douglas DC-8-54(F) Air Zaïre at Johannesburg Airport, July 1992. Air Zaïre, known as Air Congo until October 1971, was formed in June 1961 as the national airline of the Congo and operations began from Kinshasa with a Boeing 707 leased from Sabena. Apart from the extensive domestic network centred around Kinshasa and Lubumbashi, the airline scheduled regional and international services to London, Brussels, Paris and Rome, and African cities including Abidjan, Dakar, Nairobi and Douala, mainly operating Douglas DC-8-32s and Douglas DC-8-63s. This aircraft was delivered to Trans Canada Airlines as CF-TJH on January 1961 and converted to a DC-8-54(F). It served with Zantop and Kalitta before being bought by Air Zaïre in April 1992. After the demise of Air Zaïre, New Air Zaïre was created in partnership between the Zaïre government and Sabena and then reorganised under the name Lignes Aériennes Congolaises in May 1997. It was withdrawn from use and stored at Goma Airport in 1999. (Michel Anciaux)

9Q-CLV Douglas DC-8-54(F) Lignes Aériennes Congolaises at Goma International in the Democratic Republic of the Congo, 14 November 2006. Goma International, located on the northern shore of Lake Kivu, lies only 13–18km south of the crater of the active volcano Mount Nyiragongo, which erupted in 2012. This DC-8-54(F) got stuck on the ramp for almost five years – the lava overran the only taxiway, so the DC-8 could not leave. Initially, the engines were run daily, but in January 2011 the ramp was cleaned, and the aircraft moved to an aeroplane cemetry near the airport. It's now a children's playground. (Guido Potters)

9Q-CLV Douglas DC-8-54(F) Lignes Aériennes Congolaises at Kinshasa N'Djili Airport, May 1998. Cockpit view. (Michel Anciaux)

CU-T1210 Douglas DC-8-43 at Cubana Port of Spain Airport, Trinidad, 18 October 1977. Cubana de Aviación is the flag carrier of Cuba. It was founded in October 1929, becoming one of the earliest airlines to emerge in Latin America. Cubana was taken over in 1959 by the new Socialist Government under Fidel Castro. The fleet already comprised Vickers Viscounts and Bristol Brittanias and in 1976 Cubana leased three Douglas DC-8-43s from Air Canada for its Canadian, Caribbean and Guyana services. Ordered by Air Canada and delivered on March 1961 as CF-TJI, it was leased to Cubana from April 1976 until February 1978, then returned to Air Canada and leased to Air Jamaica and AeroPerú. It was stored at Smyrna Airport, Tennessee, and broken up in 1983.

PH-DCI Douglas DC-8-53 KLM Royal Dutch Airlines *Sir Isaac Newton* at Amsterdam Schiphol Airport, 28 May 1975. Delivered to KLM on 3 April 1961, it left the fleet in November 1975 and was bought by VIASA as YV-131C on 10 November 1975. The aircraft was stored at Caracas Maiquetía Airport in November 1980 and bought by International Air Leases, Inc. on 5 April 1984. It was sold to Aeronaves del Perú in June 1984 and flown to Opa Locka Airport in Florida in June 1984, where it was broken up during 1985.

YV-132C Douglas DC-8-53 VIASA Venezuela at Caracas Maiquetía Airport, 30 October 1983. In early 1961, VIASA signed an agreement with KLM to operate a Douglas DC-8 on VIASA's behalf, aiming to start operations to Europe in April that year. KLM maintained a nurturing relationship with VIASA for another 24 years. VIASA went into liquidation, ceasing operations on 23 January 1997.Originally delivered to KLM as PH-DCK on 1 May 1961, this aircraft was leased to VIASA on June 1976 as YV-132C and was bought by International Air Leases on 9 March 1984 as N4980Y. It was withdrawn from use and stored at Miami Airport in March 1984. The aircraft was broken up in 1988.

C-GNDE Douglas DC-8-52 Nordair at Amsterdam Schiphol Airport, 23 September 1979. The airline operated from the 1940s until the 1980s. Initially, most of its business was international and transatlantic passenger and freight charters, using various types of aircraft such as the C-46 ,DC3, DC4, L-1049H, L-188, FH-227 and DC-8 for flights to Europe and the Caribbean. It ceased operations in 1987. Ordered by Iberia as EC-ARB on 31 May 1961. This aircraft was bought by Nordair in August 1978 and sold to Oynx Aviation, Inc. in October 1983 as N4489M. It was then bought by American International Airways in February 1992, withdrawn from use and used for spares at Willow Run Airport, Detroit, during 1992.

S7-SIA Douglas DC-8-53 Seychelles International at Amsterdam Schiphol Airport, 27 December 1982. This airline commenced non-scheduled routes from the Seychelles to Basel and Cologne, on behalf of tour operator African Safari Club, with one Douglas DC-8-53 on 2 November 1982, which was replaced by a Douglas DC-8-63 in December 1983. The airline ceased operations in July 1986. Originally delivered to KLM as PH-DCN on 17 January 1962, this aircraft was leased to Nigeria Airways, Garuda and AeroPerú, returning to KLM in August 1976. It was sold to African Safari Airways as 5Y-BAS in August 1976 and leased to SIA as S7-SIA in November 1982. It was withdrawn from use and broken up at Brussels Zaventem Airport in December 1985.

PH-DCO Douglas DC-8-53 ALM Antillean Airlines, Amsterdam Schiphol Airport, 3 October 1978. Delivered to KLM on 27 June 1962, PH-DCO was leased to Garuda on March 1972, and then bought in September 1974 as PK-GEC. It was sold to KLM in February 1978 as PH-DCO and leased to ALM from October 1978 until October 1979. Bought by Gulfstream American as N121GA in October 1979, the aircraft was converted to a Douglas DC-8-53(F) and bought by Global Aircraft Sales in February 1991. It was sold to ARCA Colombia as HK-3746X on 20 February 1991, was stored at Miami Airport in October 1998 and broken up in April 1999.

HK-2587X Douglas DC-8-51(F) ARCA Colombia at El Dorado Airport, Bogotá, 22 February 1993. ARCA Colombia was formed as a private company and began a scheduled feeder service in Colombia in the late 1950s using a fleet of C-46s and Douglas DC3s. The airline undertook freight charters throughout North and South America with several DC-8 freighters, ceasing operations in 1997. Delivered to National Airlines on 6 April 1962, N875C was leased to Air Jamaica in 1972. It was bought by Braniff Airways as N812BN on 1 September 1973, sold to ARCA Colombia in February 1980 and converted to a DC-8-51(F) as HK-2587X. It was withdrawn from use and stored at Miami Airport before being broken up 2001.

N918CL Douglas DC-8-51 Capitol Air at Smyrna Airport, Tennessee, July 1984. Capitol Air was a major US North Atlantic charter operator, formed in 1946, initially to provide aircraft sales and maintenance as well as flight training services. It conducted non-scheduled charter work, especially across the Atlantic, using a large fleet of DC-8s, until filing for bankruptcy on November 1984. This aircraft was delivered to Trans Caribbean Airways in July 1962 as N8781R. It was sold to Eastern Air Lines in January 1968, bought by Interswede Aviation as SE-DCT in November 1971 and sold to Air Jamaica as 6Y-JGE before being leased to AeroPerú as OB-R1124. It was bought by Capitol Air in July 1983, stored at Smyrna Airport and broken up in July 1984.

N805CK Douglas DC-8-51(F) Kalitta Brownsville Airport, Texas, 31 March 1992. Delivered to Delta Air Lines in January 1963 as N809E, it was sold to F B Ayer in March 1981 and stored at Marana Airport, Arizona in 1982. The aircraft was bought by Maldives International Airlines as 8Q-CA003 in August 1984. When the aircraft was with Air Maldives in January 1985, it took the registration 8Q-PNB. It was stored at Male Maldives Airport in 1986 and bought by Connie Kallita Services (later named American International Airways in March 1991) on 5 May 1987 and was leased to Trans Continental Airlines in December 1994. It returned to American International Airways in January 1997, was withdrawn from use and stored at Oscoda Airport, Michigan, in January 1997.

N253FA Douglas DC-8-43 Sterling Philippines *The Shepherd* at Marana Pinal Airport, Arizona, April 1979. The airline was a subsidiary of Sterling Airways of Denmark and was formed in 1974. It started operations in October 1975, providing passenger charter flights from Manila to Hong Kong and other destinations in the Far East. It operated three DC-8s and one SE.210 Caravelle until ceasing operations in June 1981. This aircraft was delivered to Alitalia as I-DIWG on 21 May 1963 and sold to F B Ayer in December 1976 as N253FA. It was then leased to Sterling Philippines (renamed Summit Philippines in June 1981) on 14 May 1979 as RP-C349. The DC-8 was bought in September 1982, withdrawn from use and stored at Manila Airport in October 1983 before being broken up during 1984.

N108RD Douglas DC-8-54F Airlift at Atlanta Airport, May 1979. Airlift was formed in 1945, as a division of the J P Riddle Company under the title Riddle Airlines in March 1946, with a fleet of ten Curtiss C-46s. Cargo operations started a year later with non-scheduled flights to Puerto Rico, which continued until 1956 when regular services were introduced. Extensive passenger and cargo services operated throughout the United States, Central and South America and the Caribbean using DC-8-32Fs/54Fs and 63CFs. It ceased operations in 1991. Delivered to Riddle Airlines as N108RD on September 1963, this aircraft was operated by a number of airlines before being scrapped at Luanda Airport, Angola, in 2006.

N8782R Douglas DC-8-54F Trans Caribbean Airways at Curaçao Airport, Dutch Caribbean, May 1969. Originally delivered to Trans Caribbean Airways (which merged with American Airlines in May 1971) on 21 June 1963, this aircraft was leased to Seaboard World and sold to IAS Cargo Airlines as G-BDHA in February 1976. The airline merged with British Cargo Airlines in August 1979 and the DC-8 was operated by a number of Caribbean operators including Aeromar, Aerochago, Agro Air and Alas de Transporte Internacional. In September 1992, it finally flew as N426FB for Fine Air, which was renamed Fine Air Services in January 1998 and merged with Arrow Air on 26 September 2000. The aircraft was stored at Roswell Airport, New Mexico, in April 2001.

N8008F Douglas DC-8-54F Saturn Airways at Paris Le Bourget Airport, 20 March 1971. Ordered by Trans International Airlines as N8008F on 26 April 1963, it was leased to Saturn in October 1968, bought in July 1972 and sold to Air Afrique as TU-TCG in November 1974. The aircraft was sold to Airlift International as N1041W in August 1979, leased to several airliners, such as Far North Air, CF Airfreight and Agro Air International. It was bought on 13 November 1992 and leased to Fine Air in November 1992 as N57FB. The aircraft was stored at Roswell Airport, New Mexico, in December 2001.

TU-TCB Douglas DC-8-53 Air Afrique at Paris Le Bourget Airport, April 1970. Air Afrique was a Pan-African airline owned by many West African countries for most of its history. It was established as the official transnational carrier for francophone West and Central Africa, as many of these countries did not have the capability to create and maintain their own national airline. It was founded on 28 March 1961 and ceased operations in January 2002. Delivered to Air Afrique on 10 January 1964 as TU-TCB, this aircraft was leased to UTA as F-BJCB in November 1965 and returned on July 1968. It was withdrawn from use at Luxemburg Airport in August 1983 and sold to a Dutch pancake restaurant in Purmerend, being trucked to the Netherlands. It was damaged by fire and scrapped in August 2000.

HP-950 Douglas DC-8-54F International Air at Tocumen Airport, Panama City, 14 November 1983. Inair formed as a charter company in January 1967. It began regular cargo services with Curtiss C-46s to points in Central and South America and in December 1969 it received permission to serve Miami Airport. It expanded steadily and by the late 1970s had a fleet of four Douglas DC-6Bs, a Boeing 720, and a Convair-880. The first DC-8-54F arrived in July 1981 followed by the second in August 1982. The airline ceased operations in 1986. Delivered to Japan Air Lines as JA-8014 on 5 March 1965, this aircraft was sold to Inair Panama in June 1982 as HP-950. It was bought by Agro Air International in June 1985 as N55FB and leased to several airlines such as Aerochago Airlines, Tropical Airways, Belize Air International , Tampa Colombia and Fine Air. The aircraft was stored at Miami Airport in 2007.

CF-TJP Douglas DC-8-54F Air Canada Cargo at Hellinikon Airport, Athens, 8 April 1973. Ordered and delivered to Trans Canada Air Lines (renamed Air Canada in June 1964) on 25 March 1964, it was bought by United Air Leasing in March 1984 and sold to Connie Kalitta in November 1986 as N802CK. It was in service with many other airlines including Connie Kalitta Air Services, American International Airways, Millon Air and Trans Continental Airlines. It was stored at Willow Run Airport, Detroit, in July 1999 and bought by MK Air Cargo, being used for spare parts and broken up on 13 August 2009.

I-ALEC Douglas DC-8-54F Aeral at Milano Malpensa Airport, January 1979. Aeral (contraction of AERonautica ALessandrina) was a defunct private Italian airline that used an ex-Alitalia DC-8-43. The company initially concentrated on air taxi work using a fleet of Cessna 421s. In 1978 the company introduced international cargo flights to North America with two Douglas DC-8s but unfortunately ceased operations in 1980. Ordered by Alitalia on 12 March 1965 as I-DIWL, this aircraft was sold to F B Ayer on July 1976. It was converted from a DC-8-43 series to a DC-8-54(F) on November 1978 and bought by Aeral on 15 December 1978. Stored at Rome Fiumicino Airport in September 1980, it was withdrawn from use before being broken up during April 1985.

PH-DCS Douglas DC-8-55F Philippine Airlines/KLM at Amsterdam Schiphol Airport, 3 February 1977. Delivered to KLM as PH-DCS *Alfred Nobel* on 25 July 1964, it was leased to PAL from 25 February 1977 until June 1977 and bought by PAL as RP-C843 on June 1977. It was then sold to Lukim Air Service Zaïre as 9Q-CKI on 11 August 1984 before being bought by Liberia World Airlines in June 1987 as EL-AJO and based at Monrovia Airport. The DC-8-55F was then leased to Kabo Air of Nigeria from July 1988 until December 1988 before returning to LWA and sold to Cargo Plus Aviation as 3C-FNK on December 2001. It was re-registered as 3D-FNK in August 2002 and was stored as 9Q-CMG of Kinshasa Airways; it was scrapped during 2004 at Kinshasa Airport.

G-BDDE Douglas DC-8-54F IAS Cargo Airlines at Amsterdam Schiphol Airport, 22 February 1979. IAS was formed in 1966 and began flying operations with Bristol Brittanias in 1972. It became a jet operator in the early 1970s with several DC-8s, and in August 1979, it merged with TMAC to create British Cargo Airlines (BCA). The new BCA only had a brief life: it folded in March 1980. Ordered by Trans Caribbean Airways (which merged with American Airlines in May 1971) and delivered in December 1963 as N8783R, this aircraft was stored at Fort Worth in June 1971 and bought by IAS Cargo on 20 July 1975 as G-BDDE. It ended with Fine Air in 1993, being broken up in 2001 at Opa Locka Airport.

N8783R Douglas DC-8-54F Seaboard World Airlines (SWA) at Hellinikon Airport, Athens, 6 April 1973. SWA was a major transatlantic cargo carrier. Irregular operations started on 10 May 1947, with transatlantic flights using a single Douglas DC-4. The airline introduced the first of its turbo-prop Canadair CL-44s, which were replaced during 1966 by Douglas DC-8 freighters. It also had Boeings, 707 and 747, in its fleet. Operations ceased in October 1980 when it merged with Flying Tiger Line. This aircraft was bought by Aeromar Airlines as HI-427 in November 1983. The airline merged with Aerochago in February 1986, and the DC-8-54F was leased to Interamericana de Aviación as YV-447C in October 1988. It was returned to Agro Air in April 1993 as N427FB and leased to Fine Air in January 1998. It was withdrawn from use at Opa Locka Airport, Florida, and broken up in June 2001.

9Q-CSJ Douglas DC-8-54F Sicotra Aviation at Ostend Airport, January 1987. Delivered to Air Canada as CF-TJQ on 27 August 1964, it was stored at Marana Airport in Arizona in January 1983 and bought by United Air Leasing Corp. on 6 March 1984. Zaïre Cargo bought it as 9Q-CDM in October 1984, followed by Sicotra Aviation in January 1987. It was then sold to Liberia World Airlines as EL-AJQ in July 1988, leased to ARCA Colombia from November 1991 until 1992 and finally bought by Zuliana Air in March 1994 as YV-499C. The aircraft was stored at Maracaibo in Venezulea on April 1997.

5N-AVY Douglas DC-8-51 Intercontinental at Stansted Airport, April 1984. It was delivered to Delta Air Lines on 15 May 1964 and sold to F B Ayer & Associates, Inc. on 2 September 1977. Philippine Airlines bought the DC-8-51 as RP-C830 on 24 November 1977, which leased it to Intercontinental Airlines from Nigeria on 6 June 1982. During a flight from Lagos to London Stansted Airport, the pilot missed the approach due to fog at Stansted. While overshooting, the aircraft struck another DC-8-63AF (N786FT), which was parked on the cargo apron, causing substantial damage to both DC-8s. A diversion was made to Manchester Airport where the aircraft landed safely on 5 September 1982. It was broken up at Stansted Airport on August 1984.

RP-C831 Douglas DC-8-51 Philippine Airlines at Manila Airport in the Philippines, November 1979. Originally delivered to Delta Air Lines on 24 March 1965 as N816E, it was sold to F B Ayer & Associates, Inc. on 7 December 1977 and then to Philippine Airlines as RP-C831 on 5 March 1978. Standard Aerospace bought it on January 1986. It was withdrawn from use and stored at Marana Airport in Arizona, being broken up during March 1986. (Pierre Alan Petit)

PH-DCT Douglas DC-8-55F KLM Royal Dutch Airlines at Amsterdam Airport Schiphol, 5 April 1974. White top livery! Delivered to KLM on 15 August 1964, *Pierre de Coubertin* was leased to Nigeria Airways from June 1971 until August 1971. Its next lease was to VIASA Venezuela from February 1978 until May 1978 and then to Rich International Airways from 29 September 1981 until June 1983. It was bought by United Air Leasing Corporation as N29953 in July 1983 and then Sold to National Airlines in January 1984. It was broken up during 1984.

Left: 9G-MKC Douglas DC-8-55F MK Air Cargo at Ostend Airport, 2 May 1997. Delivered to Seaboard World Airlines on 21 June 1964 as N801SW, it was leased to Transcarga Venezuela from March 1969 until April 1969. The Forces Aériennes Française bought it as 45692-F-RAFB on August 1969, and it was operational with the French Air Force until January 1983. The aircraft was sold to the Government of Togo as 5V-TAF and then bought by MK Air Cargo (renamed MK Airlines in December 1994) in January 1993 as 9G-MKC and stored at Manston Kent International Airport, where it was broken up.

Below: TC-JBZ Douglas DC-8-52 Bursa Hava Yollari at Maastricht Beek Airport in the Netherlands, 21 May 1981. Originally delivered to United Air Lines on 17 April 1965 as N8060U, it was bought by Bursa Hava Yollari in June 1980 as TC-JBZ. The aircraft was withdrawn from use at Maastricht Beek Airport in March 1981 and broken up during May 1985. The airline ceased operations because it was not granted permission to fly from the Turkish Civil Aviation Authority. All three of its DC-8s were stored at Maastricht Beek Airport: TC-JBV, -JBY and -JBZ.

PH-ADA Douglas DC-8-52 Air New Zealand at Amsterdam Schiphol Airport, 13 September 1969. It was leased from Air New Zealand from 27 May 1969 until 20 September 1969. KLM lost PH-DCH, a Douglas DC-8-53, during a hangar fire on 29 June 1968; the aircraft was completely destroyed. PH-ADA was delivered to Air New Zealand on 19 July 1965 as ZK-NZA, it was leased to KLM in 1969, where it operated in a hybrid scheme comprising Air New Zealand tail livery with KLM fuselage stripes and titles. The DC-8 was sold to Evergreen International Airlines on 24 January 1977 as N801EV and leased to North Eastern International Airways from March 1982 until February 1984. It returned to Evergreen, was withdrawn from use and stored at Marana Airport in 1987.

N42920 Douglas DC-8-52 ex-Crownair at Opa Locka Airport, Florida, 21 November 1990. Delivered to Air New Zealand on 17 September 1965 as ZK-NZC, it was bought by Howard Golden in September 1987 as N42920 and leased to Crownair in October 1988 as C-FCRN. The aircraft returned in February 1989 and was re-registered to F B Air in May 1990 as N42920. It was leased to Faucett as OB-1421 in November 1990, stored at Opa Locka Airport and converted to a DC-8-52(F) before being leased to San Air as HK-3974X in December 1994. It was seized by the US Drug Enforcement Administration on 22 December 1994, stored at Opa Locka Airport and leased to TCA do Brasil as PP-TPC. The aircraft was withdrawn from use at Manaus Airport in July 2004.

9T-TCN Douglas DC-8-55(F) Congolese Air Force at Kinshasa N'Djili Airport, Democratic Republic of the Congo, 8 December 2018. It was ordered by SAS and delivered on 27 April 1965 as SE-DBD, Its long list of operators include Swissair, Scanair, TAE, ONA, Icelandair, Kabo Air and Overnight Cargo. It was bought by MK Airlines as 9G-MKE, which converted the DC-8-55(F) to a freighter in March 1995 and sold it to Congo Airlines in 2007 as 9Q-CAQ. It was withdrawn from use at Kinshasa Airport and sold to the Congolese Air Force in 2018 as 9T-TCN, where it resumed active flying. It was not active in 2022. (Michael Ward)

PH-DCW Douglas DC-8-55F Surinam Airways at Miami Airport, 15 January 1982. Originally delivered to Philippine Airlines as PI-C802 on 25 August 1965, it was bought by KLM Royal Dutch Airlines on 19 December 1967 as PH-DCW and leased to Surinam Airways from 30 December 1979 until August 1981. Bought off lease, it was sold on 11 November 1983 to Boreas Corp. as N4809E and then leased to several other airlines such as Arrow Air, Soundair, Worldwide Air Charter, American International Airways and finally Kitty Hawk International as N6161M on 3 February 1999. The aircraft was stored at Greenville Mid-Delta Airport in Mississippi in December 1999 and was broken up and used for parts on 30 July 2013.

ST-AJD Douglas DC-8-55(F) Trans Arabian Air Transport at Addis Ababa Bole International Airport, 21 January 1988. Delivered to Japan Air Lines as JA8016 on 14 February 1966, it was sold to United Air Leasing Corp. as N907R in July 1980 and converted to a freighter in November 1980. It was bought by Orbis Travel in July 1983 and leased by Trans Arabian as ST-AJD in January 1985. Since then, it has been leased to Trans Continental, Emery, American Interntional Airways, TMC Airlines and bought by MK Airlines as 9G-MKT on 3 May 2002. It was stored at Maastricht Airport in November 2002 and left to go to Bristol Filton Airport in June 2004. The aircraft was seen at Johannesburg in 2008 as 9Q-CHM of Hewa Bora Airways.

PH-DCV Douglas DC-8-55, KLM Royal Dutch Airlines at the old Schiphol Airport, Amsterdam, September 1966. It was delivered to KLM on 19 August 1966 and sold to Garuda Indonesian Airways as PK-GJN on 21 March 1974. It was re-registered as PK-GEB in May 1974, withdrawn from use and stored at Jakarta Airport in April 1980, being bought by Omega Air, Inc. in May 1986 as N226V. The aircraft was flown to Shannon Airport in Ireland and broken up in September 1987.

N902R Douglas DC-8-55(F) Volcanair and 9Q-CKI DC-8-55F, Lukum Air Services at Ostend Airport, 27 October 1986. Delivered to SAS as LN-MOH on 8 February 1966, it was leased to Swissair and Scanair between 1971 and 1980 before being bought by United Air Leasing Corp. It was leased to Overseas National Airways and Saudi Arabian Airlines and converted to an freighter in May 1981. Rich International Airways bought it as N902R in January 1983 and sold it to National Airlines on 30 August 1985. Following lease to Volcanair in August 1986, the aircraft was bought as N807CK by Connie Kallita Services (renamed American International Airways and later Kitty Hawk International in February 1999) on 13 April 1988. It was stored at Greenville Airport , Mississippi, and broken up at Victorville Airport, California, on 22 August 2013.

HK-2632X Douglas DC-8-54(F), Líneas Aéreas del Caribe at Miami Airport, October 1982. It was delivered to VIASA on 4 November 1965 as YV-C-VID and then bought by AeroPerú as OB-R1083 on 15 July 1974. It was sold to Douglas, converted to a freighter and bought by Trans Meridian Air Cargo as G-BTAC in July 1977; the airline merged with British Cargo Airlines in August 1979. The aircraft was bought by LAC Colombia as HK-2632X in April 1981, sold to ATC as PP-TNZ in March 1998, leased to Transportes Charter do Brasil and returned in December 1999. It was withdrawn from use and stored at São Paulo Airport before being scrapped in 2004.

PH-DCZ Douglas DC-8-55F KLM Royal Dutch Airlines Cargo at Amsterdam Airport Schiphol, 21 August 1980. It was delivered to SAS as OY-KTC on 19 March 1966 and bought by KLM Cargo on 29 April 1970. The aircraft was then sold to Inair Panama in July 1981 as HP-927 and then bought by Boreas Corporation in October 1984 as N855BC. The aircraft has been sub-leased to numerous other airlines: Canafrica Transportes Aéreos, Nationair, Aero Uraguay and Connie Kallita Services and was sold to Lexus Leasing Anstalt as 9G-MKA in February 1991. It was leased to MK Airlines and then stored at Manston Airport in August 2001. The Dutch aviation museum, Aviodrome, in Lelystad, tried to save it but could not raise the funds, so it was scrapped in December 2013.

TR-LVK Douglas DC-8-55F Air Gabon Cargo at Salisbury Airport, Rhodesia (now Zimbabwe), April 1981. Delivered to Capitol International Airways on 30 November 1965 as N4905C, it was leased to Eastern Air Lines from 3 December 1965 until 30 April 1966 and leased again to Seaboard World Airlines from 13 January 1967 until July 1967 before returning to Capitol. It was bought by Air Gabon Cargo on 26 April 1975 as TR-LVK, leased to Affretair in February 1976 and re-registered as Z-WSB on 25 March 1989. On 28 January 1998, during a flight from Johannesburg to Harare in Zimbabwe, the aircraft overran the runway in heavy rain; the nose landing gear collapsed and it was damaged beyond repair.

N8072U Douglas DC-8-71 Líneas Aéreas Paraguayas (LAP) at Frankfurt Airport, 15 August 1991. Originally delivered as a DC-8-61 to United Air Lines as N8072U on 17 February 1968, it was converted to a DC-8-71 in February 1984 and bought by GPA Group Ltd in May 1990. The aircraft was then leased to LAP from 12 June 1991 until 1 June 1992 as N8072U and returned to GPA Group before being leased again to Translift Airways as EI-TLD from June 1992 until 4 November 1993. It returned to GPA Group and was transferred to AeroUSA as N500MH. It was converted to a freighter in July 1994, leased to Emery Worldwide Airlines from August 1994 until June 2000 and bought by Aeroturbine on 31 March 2003 as N500MH. It was stored at Roswell Airport, New Mexico, and broken up.

N804SW Douglas DC-8-55F Challenge Air Transport at Miami Airport, 18 October 1981. Delivered to Flying Tiger Line on 29 September 1965 as N804SW, it was directly leased to Seaboard World Airlines until December 1968, then leased to Transcarga as YV-C-VIM from 1 January 1969 until June 1975. The aircraft was leased to several other airlines, including EFS Bahamas, IAS Cargo Airlines, Challenge Air Transport, MPA Pacific Cargo and Northern Peninsula Fisheries. It was bought by Connie Kalitta Services (later renamed Kitty Hawk International) on 2 February 1987 as N801CK and withdrawn from use at Oscoda Airport Michigan. It was broken up in 2013.

TF-LLK Douglas DC-8-55F Loftleider Icelandic at Amsterdam Airport Schiphol, 23 May 1973. It was delivered to Flying Tiger Line on 13 November 1965 as N802SW and directly leased to Seaboard World Airlines. It returned from SWA and was sold to International Aerodyne in October 1969, then leased to International Air Bahama Trans Mediterranean Airways and Loftleider in October 1971 and bought by Martinair Holland on 21 September 1973 as PH-MBH. The aircraft was then leased to Garuda Indonesia Airways in December 1974. On 4 December 1974, during a Hajj flight from Surabaya Airport in Indonesia via Colombo to Jeddah, it crashed into Saptha Kanya Mountain at an altitude of 4,355ft, 40nm east of Colombo Airport in Sri Lanka.

VP-WMJ Douglas DC-8-55F Affretair at Amsterdam Airport Schiphol, June 1982. Originally ordered by Flying Tiger Line on 17 March 1966 as N803SW, it was leased to Seaboard World Airlines from March 1966 until April 1970. After returning to International Aerodyne, Inc., it was sold to Affretair in October 1972 as TR-LQR and leased to Cargoman as A40-PA from 20 January 1977 until June 1982. It returned to Affretair as VP-WMJ and was re-registered as Z-WMJ in November 1983, before being bought by Transair Cargo in November 1997 as 3D-KRU. The aircraft was re-registered as 9Q-CDG in May 1998 for Continental Cargo Airlines in June 1998 and bought by Trans Air Cargo Services as 9Q-CJC in April 2005. It was broken up at Kinshasa N'Djili Airport. (Peter de Groot)

TR-LQR Douglas DC-8-55F Affretair at Hellinikon Airport, Athens, 8 April 1973. Affretair was formed as a Gabon-based associate cargo company of Air Trans Africa. Its first Douglas DC-8-55F was bought on 9 October 1972 for overseas freight operations. This was part of the Rhodesian 'sanctions busting' operations, where high-quality Rhodesian beef was flown by a Douglas DC-7C (VP-YTY) to Gabon by Air Trans Africa and then carried by Affretair to European destinations. During the 1980s, Affretair operated two Douglas DC-8-55F aircraft on cargo flights to Europe and within Africa. It was taken over by Air Zimbabwe in 1983.

PH-MAS Douglas DC-8-55F Martinair at Amsterdam Airport Schiphol, 15 January 1977. It returned from a lease to Iran Air in basic Martinair colours and was delivered to Overseas National Airways as N851F on 20 June 1966. It was bought by Martinair Holland as PH-MAS on 22 November 1968, and leased to several operators such as UTA, Garuda Indonesia and Iran Air between October 1971 and October 1976. Sold to Douglas on 14 January 1977 as N5824A, it was then leased to KLM as PH-MAS from April 1977 until September 1977 and sold to Aviaco in October 1977 as EC-DBE. The aircraft was bought by ARCA Colombia on 14 April 1988 as N5824A, leased to Andes Airlines from Ecuador in December 1989 and returned to G&B Aviation in December 1990. It was then leased by ARCA in January 1992. The aircraft was withdrawn from use and broken up at Miami Airport in December 1998.

N819SL Douglas DC-8-55 Holidair at Miami Airport, November 1991. Originally delivered to Japan Air Lines as JA8017 on 27 September 1966, it was bought by Overseas National Airways as N910R in June 1980 and directly leased to Saudi Arabian Airlines until April 1985. It was in use with several operators, such as Alia Royal Jordanian, Boreas Corp, Gamair, and Export Air as 5N-AUS in September 1988. Holidair Airways bought it as C-FFKD in December 1988 and sold it to Antares Aircraft in May 1989 as N81906. It was leased to Holidair and withdrawn from use at Calgary. It then returned to Antares as N819SL and was leased to Hispaniola Airways from September 1991 until February 1993, where it was bought by African International Airways as 3D-AIA in May 1994. The aircraft was broken up at Luxemburg Findel Airport in December 1995.

PH-MAU Douglas DC-8-55F Martinair Holland at Amsterdam Airport Schiphol, 13 May 1977. Delivered to ONA as N852F on July 1966, it was bought by Martinair Holland on 1 October 1969 as PH-MAU and then sold to Aviaco as EC-DEM in November 1978. It was bought by World Wide Air Charter Transport as C-FDWW in December 1986, leased to American International Airways in January 1993 as N6161C and then bought off lease by the airline (renamed Kitty Hawk International in February 1999) in October 1995. The aircraft was withdrawn from use in April 2000 at Oscoda Airport, Michigan, and broken up in May 2002.

EC-DEM Douglas DC-8-55F *Goya* Aviación y Comercio S A (Aviaco) at Amsterdam Airport Schiphol just before its delivery flight to Madrid from Martinair Holland on 17 November 1978. Aviaco was formed on 18 February 1948 by a group of Bilbao businessmen to operate all-cargo services with a fleet of Bristol 170 Freighters. Scheduled passenger services were added in 1950, linking several cities in Spain, followed by flights to the Canary Islands. It bought Convair CV-440s from Sabena in 1959 and started a vehicle ferry service to Palma with two ATL Carvairs in 1964. The fleet was growing with Fokker F27s, Caravelles, DC-9s and DC-8-52s/55s and DC-8-63s. The airline ceased operations on 1 September 1999.

5N-ATY Douglas DC-8-55F Flash Airlines at London Stansted Airport, 7 April 1987. First flown on 22 July 1966, it was delivered to Panagra Airways in September 1966 as N1509U. The airline merged with Braniff International Airways in February 1967 and the DC-8-55F was sold to Canadian Pacific as CF-CPT *Empress of Santiago* in November 1967. It was bought by IAS Cargo International Aviation Service on 15 February 1978 as G-BSKY, stored at Hurn Airport in March 1980 and bought by Andes as HC-BJT on 17 February 1982. In August 1985 it was sold as 3D-ADV to African International Airways, which then sold it to Flash Airlines in April 1987. It was next bought as EL-AJQ by Liberia World in September 1993 and sold to Cargo Plus in 2001 as 3C-QRG. Kinshasa Airways bought the DC-8 in 2003 as 9Q-CAN and sold it to Hewa Bora Airways in September 2007.

5N-ARH Douglas DC-8-55F ARAX Airlines at Amsterdam Airport Schiphol, 22 February 1986. Originally delivered to KLM as PH-DCU *Sir Winston Churchill* on 26 February 1966, it was leased to Philippine Airlines and Rich International between May 1976 and June 1981. It was bought by Orbis Travel Agency as N29954, leased to Trans Arabian Air Transport and Transafrican Air Cargo and sold to ARAX Airlines as 5N-ARH on 22 November 1985. On a flight from Cairo Airport to Sharjah Airport in the UAE, on 31 March 1988, one of the DC-8 engines caught fire on its second take-off attempt; the DC-8 crashed on the runway at Cairo Airport and was damaged beyond repair.

163050 EC-24 United States Navy, Greensboro Piedmont Triad International, North Carolina, 29 January 1994. It was ordered by United Airlines as a DC-8-54F, registered as N8048U, on 28 September 1966, and then bought by the Electrospace Systems, Inc. on 13 November 1984, before being sold to the US Navy in June 1987 as 163050. Extensive fitting of electronic countermeasures equipment was carried out before the aircraft was operated on behalf of the US Navy. It was assigned to the Electronic Warfare Support Group to provide specialised electronic warfare training. It made several visits to the UK and the Netherlands and was withdrawn from use and stored at Davis-Monthan Air Force Base in Arizona on 12 December 1998. It is preserved on 'Celebrity Row' at Davis-Monthan Air Force Base.

N806SW Douglas DC-8-55F Inex Adria Airways at Amsterdam Airport Schiphol, 23 May 1972. Inex Adria Airways was established in 1968 as the successor to Adria Aviopromet (founded in March 1960), which had began charter operations with a fleet of four ex-KLM Douglas DC-6Bs. It also flew charter and inclusive-tour flights into Ljubljana and Dubrovnik from various parts of Europe. From 1972, during the busy summer season it leased a SE-210 Caravelle and Douglas DC-8-55F, which were later replaced by Douglas DC-9s. Delivered to Seaboard World Airlines on 20 October 1967 as N806SW, ths aircraft was in use with many other airliners like Air Afrique, Trans Continental, American International Airways and TMC Airlines. It was broken up at Willow Run Airport, Michigan, in 2004.

EC-DYA Douglas DC-8-54F Air Cargo Spain at Amsterdam Airport Schiphol, 15 April 1986. Delivered to United Air Lines on 19 March 1968 as N8051U, it was sold to PK Finans International in July 1985, leased to Air Cargo Spain on 19 July 1985 and bought in November 1985. It was then sold to Aviation Leasing Group in May 1987 and withdrawn from use at Madrid–Barajas Airport before being leased to Buffalo Airways as N925BV and Baku Express in February 1997 as 4K-555. It was bought on April 1997 and leased to Cougar Airways as EL-WVD in November 1997. On 18 November 1997, the DC-8 was flying to Mwanza Airport in Tanzania from Entebbe Airport in Uganda to collect 40 tons of frozen fish fillets when it crashed during three missed approaches at night, even though Mwanza was a daytime-operations-only airport. It was damaged beyond repair. (Peter de Groot)

N8776 Douglas DC-8-61 Capitol International Airways, still in the colours of Eastern Airlines at Amsterdam Airport Schiphol, 23 June 1971. Originally delivered to Eastern Airlines on 16 May 1967, it was leased to Capitol from June until October 1967 and bought by Japan Airlines in June 1973 as JA8060. It has been operated by a considerable number of airlines including Canafrica, Trans International Airlines, Sudan Airways, Aviateca, and Agro Air International in July 1993 as N30UA. It was leased to Fine Air, which merged with Arrow Air in September 2000, and then leased to Interflight and to Bismillah Airlines as S2-AEK on 28 October 2004. It was broken up at Opa Locka Airport, Florida, in 2012.

N1804 Douglas DC-8-62 Braniff International at Lima Airport, Perú, 8 December 1973. It was delivered to Braniff International Airways on 20 September 1967 as N1804 and sold to International Air Leases in November 1983. It was then leased to Arrow Air, Rich International, Líneas Aéreas Paraguayas and returned to Arrow Air on 15 January 1991. It was sub-leased to Ansett Air Freight from July 1994 until April 1995 and leased again to Arrow Air in June 1995. On 13 December 2002, while being operated by Fine Air, on a flight from Yokota Air Force Base, Tokyo, to Changi International Airport, Singapore, the DC-8 landed in heavy rain, overrunning the runway. It came to rest about 300m from the end of the runway, damaged beyond repair.

EC-CCG Douglas DC-8-61CF Spantax S A at Düsseldorf Airport, 3 October 1980. It was bought by Trans Caribbean Airways and delivered on 28 December 1967 as N8787R. It merged with American Airlines in May 1971 and leased to Trans Caribbean Airways from May 1971 until January 1973. It was sold to Spantax S A on 25 February 1973 as EC-CCG and bought by Guinness Peat Aviation on 22 October 1984 and leased to United Parcel Service on 15 November 1984. It was re-registered as N8787R and bought in March 1985. The aircraft was then converted to a DC-8-71CF and given a new registration, N798UP, in December 1985 before being sold to AerSale, Inc. in 1988. Its registration was cancelled in July 2010, and it was broken up at Roswell, New Mexico.

N1805 Douglas DC-8-62 Calder/Braniff International at Quito Airport, Ecuador, 30 October 1977. It was ordered by Pan American Grace but was not taken up and subsequently bought by Braniff International on 29 September 1967 as N1805. It was sold to International Air Leases in October 1983, leased to Rich International on 31 October 1983, sub-leased to Air Florida on 5 November 1983 and returned to Rich International Airways in March 1984. The aircraft was then bought by Rich International in September 1985 and leased to Pegasus International Travel Club from April 1989 until June 1990. It was returned to Rich International, withdrawn from use and stored at Miami Airport before being bought by Universal Aerogat LLC in November 1997. It was broken up at Miami Airport.

N1805 Douglas DC-8-62 Calder/Braniff Intenational, flight BN911 from Quito Airport, Ecuador, to Lima Airport, Perú, 30 October 1977. Shortly affther take-off from Quito Airport, we passed over the Chimborazo Mountain peak in central Ecuador in the Cordillera Ocidental region of the Andes. Rising to 20,702ft (6,310m), this inactive volacno with many craters is the highest peak in Ecuador; it is heavily glaciated and capped with eternal snow. We had a great view from the DC-8. The captain told us it was the perfect day to for this great view, as it is normally covered in clouds.

Below and opposite above: N1805 Douglas DC-8-62 Calder/Braniff International at Tocumen Airport, Panama City, 11 December 1973. Braniff International aircraft always had colourful schemes, but this one took things a stage further. It was given an all-over colourful design by the artist Alexander Calder, which saw the beginning of a revolution in aircraft liveries. Alexander Calder was born on 22 July 1898 in Lawnton, Pennsylvania, US, and died on 11 November 1976. He was an American artist best know for his innovative approach of using paint on a aircraft for marketing purposes. While perhaps not to everyone's taste, few could argue that it was not striking and attention-getting, especially in the Latin American market where the DC-8 was used routinely. Literally an original work of art, each side was different, and, in addition, the artist's signature appeared as identification, rather than the carrier's name. Besides the Calder DC-8-62 of Braniff, he also painted a Braniff Boeing B727-291, N408BN, in a 'Sneaky Snake' design.

Below: PH-DEB Douglas DC-8-63 KLM Royal Dutch Airlines at Amsterdam Airport Schiphol, 10 September 1980. KLM was the first customer to order 11 DC-8-63s. PH-DEA made the first flight on April 1967 but, because Douglas needed this DC-8-63 for test flights, it was not the first DC8-63 to arrive at Amsterdam Airport Schiphol. Delivery was on 8 November 1967 and, instead, PH-DEB was the first to arrive on 15 July 1967. After 17 years in service, it was bought by ATASCO Leasing, Inc. on 12 June 1984 as N929R and leased to Capitol Air on 13 June 1984. More leases followed, to National Airlines, Rosenbalm, Emery, ABX Air and Airborne Express. The aircraft was written off during a test flight from Greensboro Airport when it struck mountainous terrain west of Narrows, Virginia, on 22 December 1996.

C-GNDA Douglas DC-8-61 Nordair at Dorval Airport, Monteal, June 1978. It was delivered to Trans International Airlines on 16 June 1967 as N8961T and leased to Universal Airlines and Saber Air of Singapore in 1971. It was bought by Nordair on 21 October 1974 as C-GNDA and leased to Air Afrique and Royal Air Maroc between 1977 and 1978 before being sold to Evergreen on 6 December 1978 as N810EV. The aircraft was then leased to Libyan Arab Airlines, Overseas National and Saudi Arabian, returning to Evergreen on 31 October 1982. It was sold to UPS in May 1985 and converted to a DC-8-71CF and re-registered as N702UP. It was withdrawn from use in 2009 and scapped at Roswell, New Mexico .

PH-DEA Douglas DC-8-63 KLM Royal Dutch Airlines arriving at Amsterdam Airport Schiphol in the old colour scheme on 29 September 1970. Ordered by KLM and delivered on 8 November 1967, it was stored at Schiphol Airport in November 1982 before being bought by Capitol Air on 2 November 1983 as N908CL. It was sold to Emery Worldwide Airlines on 26 October 1984, directly leased to Airlift International and then returned to Emery. It was converted to a DC-8-63(F) and re-registered as N950R in October 1985. The aircraft was transferred to Avtel Capital in September 2001 and stored at Smyrna County Airport, Tennessee, on 28 April 2005.

N802BN Douglas DC-8-62 Braniff International at Miami Airport, April 1982. Originally delivered to Alitalia on 28 October 1967 as I-DIWN, it was bought by Braniff in November 1978 and then sold to International Air Leases, Inc. in November 1983. It was leased to Hawaiian Airlines, Aeroméxico and Zambia Airways, then stored at Miami Airport in April 1988. The aircraft was converted to a DC-8-62F in March 1989 and leased to Arrow Air and Trans Continental in February 1998. It was bought by Arrow Air on 3 March 1999 and then sold to Aviation Parts Depot in July 2005. Exported to the Republic of the Congo on 19 June 2006 as 9Q-CJL for Trans Air Cargo Service, it was called *Road Runner* and was still active in September 2011.

9Q-CJL Douglas DC-8-62F Trans Air Cargo Service *Road Runner* at Kinshasa N'Djili Airport, 29 July 2011. Seen on a take-off run, this aircraft was withdrawn from use and stored at Kinshasa N'Djili Airport. The cheat line is inspired one used by Scandinavian Airlines (SAS) in the mid-1970s. (Guido Potters)

9G-REM Douglas DC-8-62F Kuwait Airways at Amsterdam Airport Schiphol, January 1999. This aircraft was delivered to Alitalia on 16 November 1967 as I-DIWV but has since been owned by a number of leasing companies and flown by many airlines, including DETA Mozambique, Guy American Airways, Sea & Sun Aviation, Pacific East Air, MGM Grand Air, American International Airways, Trans Continental and Kuwait Airways. It was leased to Continental Cargo Airlines as 9G-REM on 3 March 1999, and on 16 October 1999 it left Ostend Airport for Kinshasa N'Djili Airport with a technical stop at Tunis Airport. During its approach into Kinshasa Airport, the DC-8 slid off the runway and caught on fire; it was damaged beyond repair.

F-BNLE Douglas DC-8-62 Union de Transports Aériens at Paris Le Bourget Airport, 27 March 1970. Union de Transports Aériens (UTA) was formed on 1 October 1963 through the merger of UAT and Compagnie de Transports Aériens Intercontinentaux. The former was founded in November 1949 by the French shipping line Compagnie Maritime de Chargeurs Reunis and other interests, which operated services to the former French territories in West Africa, along with a route to Saigon (now Ho Chi Minh City). Compagnie de Transports Aériens Intercontinentaux was formed in June 1946 as a charter company, and, in 1956, it took over the Air France routes to Australia and New Caledonia, and UTA operated long haul services. This aircraft was delivered to UTA on 23 February 1968 and sold to Air Supply Corp as N4761G in November 1984. It was bought by Airborne Express in 1986 as N803AX and stored at Wilmington Air Park, Ohio, before being broken up on 7 April 2004.

F-BOLF Douglas DC-8-62 Linhas Aéreas de Moçambique (LAM) at Paris Charles de Gaulle Airport, June 1982. LAM was established on 26 August 1936 as DETA, flying two Rapides. It acquired three Junkers JU-52s in 1938 and by March 1952 was served by a fleet of six Doves, five Rapides, three DC-3s, two Lodestars and one JU-52 for domestic services. DETA strarted a fleet modernisation with three F-27-200s in 1961 and two B737-200s were ordered in 1968. DETA was Mozambique's flag carrier until 1980 when the airline was restructured and renamed LAM. Originally delivered to UTA on April 1968 as F-BOLF, this aircraft was leased to LAM from 1 April 1981 until March 1983 and sold to Air Traffic Service as N728PL. It was converted to a DC-8-62F, transferred to Air Transport International and withdrawn from use at Piedmont Airport, North Carolina, in February 2005.

C-GMXY Douglas DC-8-62 Nationair Canada at Montreal Dorval Airport, 27 October 1985. Delivered to Swissair on 2 January 1968 as HB-IDF, it was sold to TRATCO in October 1983 as N923CL and leased to Capitol Air, Nationair and Zambia Airways. Bought by Buffalo Holdings in November 1993, it was converted to a DC-8-62(F) in May 1994, leased to Buffalo Airways and stored at Smyrna Tennessee in 1996. The aircraft was then leased to Cargo Lion on July 1998 as LX-TLC and withdrawn from use at Chateauroux Airport in France before being leased to Silk Way Airlines in July 2002 as 4K-AZ25, returning in September 2003. It was bought by Johnsons Air as 9G-RMF, stored and broken up at Ostend Airport during November 2003.

SE-DBG Douglas DC-8-62 SAS/Scanair at Zürich Kloten Airport, 6 February 1982. Originally delivered to SAS on 11 January 1968, it was leased to Scanair, a Scandinavian charter consortium with many flights in the holiday centres arround the Mediterranean, the Canary Islands, Switzerland, Gambia and Sri Lanka from October 1977 until May 1982. It was bought by United Air Leasing in October 1986 as N756UA and converted to a DC-8-62(F) in December 1986 as N729PL. More airlines leased it, including Airborne Express, Interstate Airlines, Air Transport International and finally Cargosur in January 1989 as EC-230. The aircraft was bought in April 1989 as EC-EMX. It served some time with Iberia. The aircraft was sold to Cygnus Air in November 1998. It was bought by Compagnie Africaine d'Aviation (CAA) as 3X-GEP in August 2008, and re-registered as 9Q-CHB. It was stored and scrapped at Johannesburg Airport in 2008.

OY-SBK Douglas DC-8-63 Sterling Skyliner at London Stansted Airport, 26 May 1985. First flown on 8 July 1968 and bought by SAS as LN-MOU on 16 August 1968, it was sold to Thai Airways on 22 March 1974 as HS-TGX. Sterling Airways bought it on April 1984, but it returned to SAS on October 1986 and was then leased to Scanair. It was bought by Aerolease as N794AL, leased to Trans Ocean Airways in May 1989 and converted to a DC-8-63(F) in July 1990 before being leased to Burlington Air Express on 31 July 1990. While flying cargo for Air Transport International from Seattle Airport to Toledo Airport in Ohio, the aircraft was destroyed during the approach 5km north-west of Toledo Airport on 15 February 1992.

EI-CGO Douglas DC-8-63(F) Aer Turas at Maastricht Beek Airport, 24 September 2002. Delivered to SAS on 18 September 1968 as SE-DBH, it was leased to Thai Airways International in March 1974 and bought in November 1974 as HS-TGZ. It was used by Icelandair and Air Algerie between 1982 and 1983 and bought by Sterling Airways as OY-SBM. Scanair leased it as SE-DBH from June 1986 until November 1988; it returned to Aerolease and was converted to a DC-8-63(F) in April 1989 before being bought by Aer Turas as EI-CGO on 25 April 1989. It was then leased to Saudi Arabian Airlines from May 1989 until February 1996, returned to Aer Turas in April 1998 and finally bought by First International Airways as 9G-NHA in December 2003. The aircraft was broken up at Lagos Airport in Nigeria on January 2013.

LX-TLB Douglas DC-8-62 Cargo Lion at Sharjah Airport, UAE, 6 November 1995. It was delivered to Swissair on 24 February 1968 as HB-IDG and bought by TRATCO in September 1983. Following its lease to Capitol Air in October 1983 as N922CL, it was bought in July 1984 and leased to Nationair as C-GMXR. It returned in April 1986, and another lease followed to Pluna Uruguay as CX-BQN on 24 October 1991. The aircraft was returned in October 1992 and leased to Buffalo Airways as N922BV on November 1992 before being bought by Cargo Lion LX-TLB on 3 April 1995. It was converted to a DC-8-62(F) in August 1995, stored at Châteauroux-Centre Airport, France, in March 2001 and was ferried in October 2001 to Manston Airport in the UK for scrapping.

LX-TLB Douglas DC-8-62(F) Cargo Lion at Sharjah Airport, UAE, 6 November 1995. Starting up!

CF-CPP Douglas DC-8-63 CP Air *Empress of Honolulu* at Amsterdam Airport Schiphol, 19 April 1977. Delivered to Canadian Pacific Airlines (CP Air) on 31 January 1968, it was leased to UTA from March 1972 until March 1973 as F-BOLJ. It then returned to CP Air and was leased to Worldways Canada as C-FCPP from March 1983 until October 1984 before being bought by Aerolease Financial Group as N783AL on 28 December 1990. The aircraft was converted to a DC-8-63(F) in July 1991, leased to Burlington Air Express in December 1991, and bought by Airborne Express and renamed as ABX Air in August 2003. It was sold to Meridian Airways on 21 July 2009 as 9G-AXD and broken up at Kotoka International Airport in Ghana in January 2015.

N4935C Douglas DC-8-63 Surinam Airways at Amsterdam Airport Schiphol, 24 February 1989. Originally delivered to Iberia on 18 September 1968 as EC-BMY, a short lease followed to Aviaco in 1981. It was sold to International Air Leases as N4935C on April 1984, leased to Rich International from June 1984 until April 1985 and bought by Surinam Airways (which named it *Stanvaste*) on 8 July 1985 as N4935C. It was repossessed on 21 November 1992 and went to Rich International, returning in January 1996. The aircraft was stored at Roswell Air Centre and sold to Northeast Airline service in March 1999. It was broken up at Opa Locka Airport, Florida, during January 2003.

N8075U Douglas DC-8-61 Arrow Air at Miami Airport, February 1984. This aircraft was first flown on 19 September 1967 and ordered by United Air Lines on 8 December 1967 as N8075U. It was leased to Arrow Air from 1 June 1983 until January 1985 and stored at Marana Airport, Arizona, before being bought by Airborne Express in June 1989 as N851AX. It went to First Tennessee Equipment Finance on September 28, 1990. It was withdrawn from use and stored at Willow Run Airport, Detroit, in December 1999 before being broken up at Wilmington Air Park in Ohio.

N8076U Douglas DC-8-71 United Air Lines at Seattle Tacoma Airport, Washington, 4 July 1986. Originally delivered to United Airlines as a DC-8-61 on 23 December 1967, this aircraft was converted to a DC-8-71 in May 1983. It was bought by GPA Group in September 1990 and leased to United Airlines from September 1990 until February 1991. A Douglas DC-8-71(F) freighter conversion began in August 1991, and it was leased to VASP Airlines on 27 August 1991 as PP-SOQ, staying with the airline until 7 June 1992. It returned to GPA Group in November 1992, was leased to Air Canada as C-FQPM in September 1993 and was returned again in May 1994. Emery Worldwide leased it as N8076U on 9 May 1994 and bought it in April 1998. On 26 April 2001, during a landing at Nashville Airport, the left main landing gear retracted. It was stored at Roswell in August 2001 and broken up.

N8955U Douglas DC-8-61CF Saturn Airways at Amsterdam Airport Schiphol, 16 June 1969. It was delivered on 28 December 1967 and leased to Seaboard World Airlines in January 1975. Further leases took place to EFS Bahamas, Trans International Airlines (TIA), Capitol and finally Flying Tiger as N862FT in February 1978. It was bought by UPS in May 1985 and converted to DC-8-71CF as N748U. On 8 February 2006, the aircraft had an in-flight fire on its approach into Philadelphia International Airport but landed safely. It was broken up in September 2006. Saturn Airways was formed in 1948. The airline acquired a fleet of Douglas DC-6s in 1965 and replaced them with Douglas DC-7Cs. Saturn operated civil and military charters with two DC-8-61CFs in 1967 and also one DC-8-54F in 1968. It ceased operations in 1976.

9XR-SD Douglas DC-8-62F Silverback Cargo Airlines at Johannesburg Airport, 11 November 2003. It was ordered by Japan Airlines on 19 July 1968 as JA8034 and later bought by Conner Airlines on 23 August 1983 as N162CA. It was then sold to Northeastern International Airways in December 1983 and was used by several airlines, such as Zantop International Airlines, Air Train, CF Air Freight and finally Emery World Airlines in November 1989 as N994CF. The aircraft was exported to Rwanda on 30 April 2002 as 9XR-SD for Silverback Cargo Airlines. It was withdrawn from use and stored at Kigali International Airport in Rwanda in 2010.

F-GDJM Douglas DC-8-62CF-H Cargo Lion/Southern Aviation at Ostend Airport, 12 April 1994. Delivered to Alitalia (which named it *Titano*) as I-DIWC on 10 April 1968, it was flown to Pinal Airpark in Arizona for storage in April 1981. It was bought by Minerve in November 1982 as F-GDJM, and the airline merged with Air Outre Mer (AOM) French Airlines in March 1992. The aircraft was leased to Cargo Lion on 1 August 1992 and then sold to the airline in March 1995 as LX-TLA. It was flown to Greenwood Airport, Mississippi, for storage, withdrawn from use and scrapped in 2004.

I-DIWQ Douglas DC-8-62CF-H Alitalia Cargo System at Pinal Airpark, Arizona, September 1982. First flown on 11 April 1968 and sold to Alitalia on 30 June 1968, this aircraft was flown to Pinal Airpark in June 1981 for storage. It was bought by Sea & Sun Aviation as N3931A in March 1983 and since then has been leased to Flying Tiger Line and Advance Air Charter as C-FHAA. It was delivered to Hawaiian Airlines as N3931A in June 1987, stored at Marana again and bought by American International Airways and re-registered as N818CK in May 1996. The aircaft was stored at Mojave Airport in California on 18 May 2000 and bought by Cargo Aircraft Management in December 2009 as N71CX. It was broken up at Mojave Airport in April 2014.

N8632 Douglas DC-8-63CF Saudia Arabian Airlines/Air Cargo at Amsterdam Airport Schiphol, 22 August 1980. Saudia Arabian Airlines was formed in 1946 by the Saudi Arabian government and began operations on 14 March 1947, linking Jeddah with Dhahran and Cairo with a fleet of Douglas DC-3s. The airline had standardised its jet cargo fleet with Boeing 707-386Cs and leased DC-8-63CFs during the 1980s. Originally ordered by Seaboard World Airlines as N8632 on September 1968, this aircraft was leased to Saudia on March 1977, and was re-registered as N773FT when the Seaboard merged with Flying Tiger Line in November 1980. It was bought by UPS in May 1984 as N866UP and converted to a DC-8-73CF in August 1984. Its registration was cancelled in April 2011 and the aircraft was scrapped at Roswell, New Mexico.

CC-CAX Douglas DC-8-71(F) Fast Air at Miami Airport, May 1993. It was delivered to United Airlines on 29 March 1968 as N8080U as a DC-8-61 and converted to a DC-8-71 in August 1983. It was bought by the GPA Group and converted to an freighter 71(F) in October 1992, then leased to Fast Air in November 1992 as CC-CAX, followed by MAS Air Cargo in August 1998. The aircraft was re-registered as N871MY by AeroUSA and stored at Roswell New Mexico in May 2002. It was sold to Promodal Cargo on 15 November 2003 as PR-GPT, withdrawn from use at Manaus Airport in Brazil in 2004 and broken up during 2012.

Z-WZL Douglas DC-8-71(F) Affretair at Harare Airport, Zimbabwe, 8 December 1993. Delivered to United Airlines on 25 June 1968 as N8085U, it was converted to a DC-8-71 in August 1982. It was then bought by the GPA Group Ltd in September 1990 and converted to a DC-8-71(F) freighter in December 1991. Affretair leased the aircraft as Z-WZL from Zimbabwe from 5 August 1992 until 10 June 1994, and it returned to the GPA Group in June 1994 as N8085U. It was leased to Emery Worldwide Airlines on 30 June 1994 and Emery bought the DC8-71(F) on 16 April 1998. It was sold to Aeroturbine, Inc. from Miami in March 2003, and it was scrapped during 2004.

HB-IDH Douglas DC-8-62CF Swissair at Hong Kong Kai Tak Airport, 25 March 1972. Originally ordered by Swissair and delivered on 11 July 1968 as HB-IDH *Piz Bernina*, it was leased to Balair from 1 April 1976 until 1978. It returned to Swissair and had a new lease in September 1979 until December 1981. After returning to Swissair, it was bought by the Fuerza Aérea del Perú as OB-1373 on 28 December 1981 and was re-registered as FAP371. It operated two DC-8-62CFs – ex-Swissair HB-IDK and -IDH, which became FAP370 and FAP371. Both flew for the presidental flight and were stored at Lima Airport in Perú and broken up during 1994.

F-BOLG Douglas DC-8-62 UTA/Air Cambodge at Paris Le Bourget Airport, 3 March 1973. Delivered to UTA on 6 June 1968 as F-BOLG, the DC-8 had small Air Cambodge titles on the front of the fuselage, probably a lease. It was bought by Finnair on 20 December 1975 as OH-LFZ and leased by Kar-Air from Finland in March 1984, which then bought it on 31 December 1985. The aircraft was sold to Airborne Express on 18 February 1987 as N804AX and sold to Tarmac Accessory Service for scrapping in 2002 at Wilmington Airport in Ohio; it was scrapped in 2005.

LX-ACV Douglas DC-8-63CF Air India Cargo at Paris Orly Airport, 18 March 1980. Originally delivered to Flying Tiger Line on 17 June 1968 as N779FT, it was bought by Cargolux as LX-ACV on 19 May 1977 and leased to Air India Cargo from September 1979 until March 1980. It was then leased to Aero Uruguay from 30 April 1981 and returned in June 1982. Aer Turas leased it in October 1982 as EI-BNA *City of Dublin* and then bought it on 2 July 1984. It was leased to Saudi Arabian Airlines from September 1989 until January 1998, and after returning to Aer Turas, it was flown to Pinal Airpark in Arizona for storage on 30 November 1999. The aircraft was broken up 2004.

LX-ACV Douglas DC-8-63CF Air India Cargo. There are five seats in the DC-8-63CF cockpit: two up front and three on a sideways double bench. (Michel Anciaux)

TF-CCV Douglas DC-8-63CF Cargolux at Rotterdam Zestienhoven Airport, February 1978. Delivered to Flying Tiger Line on 17 July 1968 as N780FT, it was bought by Cargolux on 30 June 1977 and leased to Air India Cargo in April 1983. This aircraft has quite an incredible history, as it has been operated by a considerable number of airlines: Martinair Holland, Evergreen Internationl Airlines, TNT, UPS, DHL Express, Astar Air Cargo, Skybus, Heavylift Cargo, Perúvian Airlines and Skybus Jet Cargo. It was converted to a DC-8-73CF freighter in January 1985 and is still active at the time of writing (April 2022), flying out of Miami as a Skybus Jet Cargo aircraft on a regular basis with the registration OB-2059-P.

D-ADUI Douglas DC-8-73CF German Cargo at Sharjah Airport, UAE, 10 November 1995. Bought by Flying Tiger Line and delivered on 26 July 1968 as a DC-8-63CF with the registration N781FT, it was sold to Cammacorp in August 1983 and leased to Flying Tiger Line. It was converted to a DC-8-73CF in June 1984 and sold to German Cargo on 10 July 1984 as D-ADUI. The airline was renamed Lufthansa Cargo in May 1993, and the aircraft was bought by Aerolease Financial Group on 17 June 1996 as N602AL. It was leased to Emery Worldwide Airlines on 9 September 1996, returned and leased to Air Transport International (ATI) in December 2002 and re-registered as TT-DBC of Stabo Air in December 2013. It was changed to TT-DFJ of CFS Cargo in 2015 and was withdrawn from use at Doha Airport in Qatar during June 2018.

D-ADUI Douglas DC-8-73CF German Cargo at Sharjah Airport, 10 November 1995. Close up, waiting for cargo!

9G-AXC Douglas DC-8-63(F) Meridian Airways at Ostend Airport, 10 July 2010 (9G-AXB in hangar). Originally delivered to KLM Royal Dutch Airlines on 21 July 1968 as PH-DEC *Marco Polo*, it was bought by Icelandair on 13 March 1984 as TF-FLU and leased to Trans Continental Airlines as N820TC in May 1989. It was converted to freighter and leased to several airlines: Southern World Airlines, Electra Aviation, American International Airways and Air Transport International as N787AL in October 1992. The aircraft was re-registered as N788AL, bought by ABX Air as N828AX in February 1997 and was exported to Ghana as 9G-AXC on 21 July 2009 for Meriadian Airways. It was withdrawn from use and broken up at Accra Kotoka International Airport during January 2015. (Stefaan Eerebout)

HB-IDM Douglas DC-8-63CF SA de Transport Aerien (SATA) at Geneva Airport, 31 September 1978. It was delivered on 23 September 1968 to Overseas National Airways as N863F and leased to Air Siam from 28 March 1971 until January 1972, before being sold to Flying Tiger Line in September 1973 as N799FT. SATA bought it in June 1974 as HB-IDM, keeping it until December 1978. It was used by several airliners like Trans International, Trans America and Fedex Express until the United Parcel Service bought it in July 1990 as N404FE. It was re-registered as N810UP in September 1990. The aircraft's registration was cancelled on 18 October 2010 at Louisville Airport, Kentucky, where it was stored and scrapped.

N815EV Douglas DC-8-73CF Evergreen International Airlines at Amsterdam Airport Schiphol, 18 January 1986. Delivered to Flying Tiger Line as a DC-8-63CF on 17 September 1968 as N782FT and sold to Cargolux in October 1975 as LX-BCV, it was re-registered as TF-BCV in November 1975 and leased to Evergreen International as N815EV. The airline bought it in July 1984, and it was converted to a DC-8-73CF and operated by TNT Europe and UPS from May 1992 until April 1994. It was re-registered as N815UP to DHL in June 1994 and bought by DHL in March 1995. The aircraft was re-registered as N806DH in June 1996, and stored at Kingman, Arizona, in June 2012. (Peter de Groot)

N784FT Douglas DC-8-63AF Flying Tiger Line at Hong Kong Kai Tak Airport, 24 March 1972. First flown on 17 September 1968 and bought by Flying Tiger Line as N784FT on 25 October 1968, it was converted to a DC-8-73AF in October 1982 and sold to UPS in December 1982. It was re-registered as N804UP in July 1983 and retired and scrapped at Roswell Airport on 18 June 2010. Flying Tiger Line, also known as Flying Tigers, was the first scheduled cargo airline in the US and became a major military charter operator during the Cold War era for both cargo and personnel. It used aircraft such as the Douglas C-54 ,Canadair CL-44, Boeing 707 and many DC8-63s and also Boeing 747s. It merged with Federal Express on 7 August 1989.

ST-AJR Douglas DC-8-54F Trans Arabian Air Transport (TAAT) at Amsterdam Airport Schiphol, 19 July 1986. Originally delivered to United Airlines as N8052U on 31 October 1968, it was bought by the Aviation Leasing Group on 3 June 1985 and leased to TAAT in July 1985 as ST-AJR until 1987. It was owned by a number of leasing companies and flown by many airlines, including Arcturus Aircraft , Trans Continental, Chrysler Technological Systems, American International Airways, Zantop International Airlines, and Kitty Hawk International on 7 May 1999. The aircraft was withdrawn from use and stored in April 2000 (location unknown).

`3D-ADV Douglas DC-8-54F African International at Ostend Airport, 2 May 1997. First flown on 11 October 1968, and bought by United Airlines as N8055U on 23 November 1968, it was sold to Wind CI Ltd in November 1984 and leased to Trans Sahel Airlines on 22 February 1985 as EL-AJK. It was bought by Trans Sahel in November 1986 as 5N-AWZ and sold to African International in August 1987 as 3D-ADV. The aircraft was stored at Johannesburg O R Tambo International Airport in 2004 and re-registered as ZS-PAE for African International Airways. It was withdrawn from use in 2006 at Johannesburg O R Tambo International.

N8055U Douglas DC-8-54F United Jet Freighter at Long Beach California, November 1968. Along with KLM DC-8-63 PH-DEE, Trans International Airlines DC8-63CF N4863T and two Flying Tiger Line DC-8-63CFs, all the DC-8s were delivered during November 1968. In 1957, Donald Douglas Jr took over Douglas Aircraft Company from his father. Under his leadership, production at the Long Beach plant shifted to commercial aircraft, beginning with the Douglas DC-8. The firm invested US$20 million in a plant for aircraft on the east side of Lakewood Boulevard, which opened in 1957. The 176-passenger plane, DC-8-11 N8008D, made its maiden flight from Long Beach Airport on 30 May 1958. The DC-8 and its subsequent versions held a 14-year production run in Long Beach. (Geoffrey Thomas Collection)

N782SP Douglas DC-8-72CF Samaritan's Purse at Glasgow Prestwick Airport, 10 March 2022. It had been at Glasgow Prestwick Airport about six times in the last four weeks on its way to Poland from the US. Known as a combi DC-8, it is specially configured to carry up to 84,000lb of cargo and 32 passengers, significantly increasing the organisation's capacity to respond immediately in times of crisis around the world. Originally delivered to Finnair as a DC-8-62CF on 27 January 1969, OH-LFR was re-registered as OH-LFT in April 1969. It was bought by the L'Armée de l'Air as F-RAFG on 23 November 1981 and converted to a DC-8-72CF in June 1982. It was sold to ATI on 27 June 2005 as N721CX and bought by Skybus Jet Cargo in October 2014. In March 2015, it was bought by Samaritan's Purse as N782SP. It is still active today (May 2022). (Bob Logan)

N721CX Douglas DC-8-72CF Air Transport International (ATI) at Lajes Air Base, Azores, 8 August 2011. Conducting a weekly flight from Baltimore/Washington International Airport to Lajes Air Base, the DC-8 has a passenger cabin in the rear for 32 passengers; the cargo door is at the front. The majority of the families of the US military personnel assigned to Lajes live in the housing area on the base.

TC-MAB Douglas DC-8-61 Birgenair at Paris Orly Airport, 1 May 1994. Delivered to Eastern Airlines on
15 November 1968 as N8765, it was leased to Japan Airlines on 21 November 1976 and returned in March 1976.
Other leases included to Capitol International Airways, ONA, Saudi Arabian, Capitol Air and Airlift International. It
was bought by Spantax SA on 27 October 1984 as EC-DVC and sold to BACG Finance and Leasing in June 1988,
which leased it to Atlantic Icelandic in December 1988 and sub-leased it to Birgenair in June 1989 as TC-MAB.
The aircraft was bought by ABX Air on 12 December 1994 as N852AX and broken up at Greensboro, North
Carolina, during 2003.

N1301L Douglas DC-8-61 Delta Airlines at Miami International Airport, 19 November 1980. First flown on
18 November 1968 and delivered to Delta Airlines as N1301L in December 1968, it was converted to a DC-8-71
with CFM56 engines in April 1982. It was sold to United Parcel Service on 9 December 1986 and converted to
a Freighter DC-8-71F in October 1987 as N718UP. The aircraft was bought by AerSale, Inc. on 20 May 2010,
withdrawn from use at Roswell, New Mexico, in 2010 and later scrapped.

TF-VLY Douglas DC-8-63 Icelandair/Eagle Air/leased to Air Algerie at Amsterdam Airport Schiphol, 24 September 1985. Originally delivered to KLM as PH-DEE *Abel Tasman* on 27 November 1968, it was in service for 17 years with KLM. It was leased to Eagle Air as TF-VLY on 15 April 1985 and sub-leased to Saudia on 5 May 1985, returning on 19 September 1985. It was bought by PK Finans International in October 1985, sold to International Parcel Express on 25 October 1985 as N819UP and converted to a freighter DC-8-73(F) in April 1986. It was transferred to UPS in 1998, withdrawn from use in 2009 and bought by AerSale on 29 December 2010. The aircraft was stored and withdrawn from use at Roswell, New Mexico.

PH-DEE Douglas DC-8-63 KLM Royal Dutch Airlines/VIASA at Jorge Chávez Airport, Lima, 17 December 1974. This was my flight back to Europe, operated by VIASA as flight VA735/730, with stops at Bogotá, Caracas, Madrid, London and Amsterdam and a total flying time of 15 hours, 20 minutes. In early 1961, the airline signed an agreement with KLM to operate a DC-8-32/33 on VIASA's behalf, aimed at starting operations to Europe that year.

9G-MKK Douglas DC-8-62AF MK Airlines at Hellinikon Airport, Athens, 4 August 2000. It was delivered to Japan Airlines (JAL) as JA8036 on 13 December 1968 and renamed JAL *Courier Jet Trader* in January 1988. It was sold to Con-Av Corp on 2 February 1988 as N771CA, re-registered as N36UA in May 1988 for United Aviation Service. Evergreen International bought it on 24 August 1988 as N817EV, and it was seen in use with other airlines, such as GE Engine Service, Ventures Holiday and finally Trans Continental as N187SK. The aircraft was withdrawn from use and stored at Willow Run Airport, Detroit, in January 2000. It was sold to MK Airlines on 5 May 2005, which ceased operations in June 2008, and the aircraft was stored at Kenneth Kaunda International Airport in Zambia.

EC-EMD Douglas DC-8-62 Cargosur at Las Palmas Gando Airport, 29 October 1993. Delivered to Japan Airlines as JA8035 on 11 November 1968, it was bought by the World Aircraft Sales Company in August 1984 and leased to JAL in January 1988. The aircraft was converted to a DC-8-62(AF) in July 1988, sold to Avengair in August 1988 as N731PL and leased to Interstate Airlines before returning in November 1988. It was then leased to Cargosur of Spain on 9 December 1988 as EC-217, which bought the DC-8-62AF on 9 March 1989 as EC-EMD. The airline merged with Iberia in June 1995, and the aircraft was sold to Cygnus Air and leased to Iberia. It was bought by Trans Air Congo Service in August 2008 as 3X-GEN, transferred to Trans Air Congo as 9Q-CJH and stored at Kinshasa N`Djili Airport.

ZP-CCR Douglas DC-8-61 Líneas Aéreas Paraguayas at Brussels Airport, July 1988. Originally delivered to Eastern Airlines on 19 December 1968 as N8763, it was leased to Japan Airlines from 26 September 1972 until March 1976 and then to Capitol International Airways, ONA, Airlift International, and Spantax SA as EC-DVB on 27 October 1984. Then LAP bought it on 18 January 1988 as ZP-CCR. On 5 April 1990, during a flight from Asunción to Buenos Aires, the DC-8-61 aquaplaned and slipped off the runway while landing in very bad weather at Buenos Aires Ezeiza Airport. No crew or passengers were injured. The aircraft was stored until February 1995 when it was bought by Airborne Express as N853AX. It was broken up at Wilmington Air Park, Ohio, in 2006. (Michel Anciaux)

Right: ZP-CCR Douglas DC-8-61 Líneas Aéreas Paraguayas. Flight engineer's panel. (Michel Anciaux)

Below left: ZP-CCR Douglas DC-8-61 Líneas Aéreas Paraguayas. The cabin interior, economy class. (Michel Anciaux)

Below right: ZP-CCR Douglas DC-8-61 Líneas Aéreas Paraguayas. Cockpit. (Michel Anciaux)

YV-C-VIA Douglas DC-8-63 VIASA Venezuela/KLM at Amsterdam Airport Schiphol, 25 February 1970. Delivered to VIASA on 22 December 1968 and re-registered as YV-125C in November 1975, this aircraft has been operated by a considerable number of airlines: Caribbean Airways, Icelandair, Scanair, Zambian Air Cargo, Arrow Air, Southern World Airlines, ACS Canada, CLA Air Transport, and DBA Cargo as N345JW on 10 January 2005. It was converted to a DC-8-63(F) freighter in January 1989 and stored at Roswell Air Centre, New Mexico, on 29 March 2005.

OH-LFV Douglas DC-8-62CF Finnair at Amsterdam Airport Schiphol, 16 March 1973. First flown on 8 March 1969 and delivered to Finnair O/Y as OH-LFS on 22 March 1969, it was re-registered as OH-LFV in March 1969. The DC-8-62CF was bought by the L'Armée de l'Air on 20 October 1975 as F-RAFD/46043, where it was converted to a DC-8-72CF with CFM56-2C1 engines in May 1983 and re-registrated as F-ZVMT in January 1999. It was stored at Châteaudun Air Base in France on 30 June 2004 and broken up during December 2006.

4R-EXJ Douglas DC-8-63CF Expo Aviation at Malta International Airport, 14 February 2013. Expo Aviation from Sri Lanka was established in 1997, with operations commencing in 1998 using two Antonov An-8s, which were replaced by Antonov-12s. In 2001, Expo Aviation started domestic operations to Jaffna using Ilyushin IL-18 and Antonov An-26 aircraft. Soon after, the airline was renamed ExpoAir. In 2002, the airline leased three Fokker F27s from Oman Air and an additional Ilyushin IL-18 started operating in 2003. During 2005, Expo Air applied to conduct international cargo services, and, in 2005, a DC-8-63CF was added to the fleet. Expo Aviation became Fits Air in 2013. The DC-8 flew to Nairobi in Kenya on 28 September 2013 where it was stored and put up for sale. (Jonathan Mifsud)

N8635 Douglas DC-8-63CF Seaboard World Airlines at Rhein-Main Air Base, Frankfurt, 26 August 1972. It was delivered to Seaboard World Airlines on 30 January 1969 as N8635 and leased to Korean Air Lines from 1 December 1972 until September 1975. Overseas National Airways then leased the aircraft from 10 May 1976. On 4 March 1977, during a flight from Paris Charles de Gaulle Airport to Niamey Airport in Niger for UTA Cargo, it crashed short of the runway during the approach; it was damaged beyond repair.

N31EK Douglas DC-8-63CF Connie Kalitta Services at Pinal Airpark, Marana in Arizona, December 1984. Originally delivered to Seaboard World Airline on 11 March 1969 as N8637 and leased to Korean Airlines from April 1973 until March 1974, it was bought by Transcarga on 3 June 1975 as YV-C-VIN. The aircraft was re-registered as YV-130C in November 1975 and used by VIASA until 1979. It was sold to Douglas Aircraft Company on 28 January 1982 as N2919N, then bought by Connie Kalitta on 15 February 1984 and re-registered as N31EK in June 1984. It was sold to UPS in March 1985 and converted to a DC-8- 73CF as N852UP. The aircraft was withdrawn from use in 2009 and bought by AerSale, Inc.; it was broken up at Roswell, New Mexico, in 2013.

TR-LTZ Douglas DC-8-73CF Government of Gabon at Paris Le Bourget Airport, 11 November 1983. It was first flown on 24 February 1969 and delivered to Seaboard World Airlines as a DC-8-63CF N8638 on March 1969 before being leased to Korean Airlines from April 1973 until March 1974. It was bought by the Republique Gabonaise on 27 November 1974 as TR-LTZ *Franceville* and converted to a DC-8-73CF with CFM56-2C engines in August 1982. The aircraft was stored at Nimes Airport in France and withdrawn from use in 1995.

HS-TGY Douglas DC-8-63 Thai Airways at Amsterdam Airport Schiphol, 6 May 1979. The aircraft was first delivered to SAS as LN-MOY on 26 April 1969 and bought by Thai Airways on 26 October 1974 as HS-TGY. It was sold to Sterling Airways on 9 May 1984 as OY-SBL, bought by Scanair on 31 December 1987 and sold again to Aerolease in November 1988 as N796AL. The aircraft was converted to a freighter DC-8-63(F), leased to CF Airfreight and Emery Worldwide, bought by International Air Response, Inc. on 7 July 2002 and leased to Aeropostal Cargo de Mexico as XA-TXS in June 2003. It was stored at Querétaro International Airport, Mexico, in 2010.

HB-IGH Douglas DC-8-72 Jet Aviation Business Jets at Basel International Airport, 8 October 2007. Originally delivered as a DC-8-62H to United Airlines as N8966U on 15 June 1969, it was bought by NSAR Associated, Inc. on 2 September 1983 and re-registered as VR-BJR on 15 October 1986, operating for Al Nassr Ltd, and was converted to DC-8-72 with CFM56-2C engines. It was bought by Jet Aviation Business Jets AG on September 2000 as HB-IGH and sold to Aero Turbine in December 2007 as N274AT. Brisair bought it as VP-BHS in May 2011 and then sold it to Skybus Jet Cargo as N872SJ on 14 November 2016. It was withdrawn from use at Kingman Airport, Arizona, in February 2017.

9XR-SC Douglas DC-8-62H Silverback Cargo Airlines at Amsterdam Schiphol Airport, 3 January 2005. It was delivered to United Airlines as N8967U on 15 June 1969 and sold to Zantop International Airlines on 4 December 1985. The aircraft was converted to a freighter in March 1986 and bought by Air Train, operating for CF Air Freight as N816ZA. It was then transferred to Emery Worldwide Airlines in January 1991 as N990CF and leased to Silverback Cargo Airlines on 7 May 2002 as 9XR-SC before being withdrawn from use at Kigali International Airport in Rwanda during 2010. It was broken up in 2015.

N4865T Douglas DC-8-63CF Aeroméxico *Chiapas* at Madrid-Barajas Airport, 6 August 1973. It was delivered to TIA on 22 August 1969 and leased to Aeroméxico from March 1971 until March 1974. It returned to TIA and was leased to Air Algerie and Air Afrique before being converted to a DC-8-73CF in July 1982 and leased to UPS and then Flying Tiger Line as N702FT in June 1989. When Flying Tiger Line merged with Fedex Express, the aircraft was re-registered as N402FE in January 1990. It was sold to UPS in September 1990 and registered as N803UP in November 1990. It was bought by AerSale on 26 February 2010 as N155CA, stored at Roswell Airport in June 2012 and bought by Skybus Jet Cargo on 23 March 2022.

TF-FLT Douglas DC-8-63 Icelandair at Luxemburg Airport, 19 April 1985. It was originally delivered to KLM Royal Dutch Airlines on 29 August 1969 as PH-DEH *Vasco da Gama* and sold to Icelandair on 18 March 1985 before being leased to SAS from 27 October 1985 until 22 November 1985. Electra Aviation bought it as N512FP on 23 May 1990 and leased it to Hawaiian Airlines on 29 May 1990. It returned to Electra Aviation on 18 June 1993, whereupon it was flown to Mojave Airport and stored. The aircraft was bought by the Aerolease Financial Group in July 1993, leased to Airborne Express on 1 September 1993 as N818AX and bought on 3 January 1995. It was withdrawn from use in November 2003 and stored at Wilmington Airport, Ohio. It was scrapped during 2004.

HB-IDK/370 Douglas DC-8-62CF Fuerza Aérea del Perú at Zürich Airport, 24 December 1981. First flown on 10 June 1969 and bought by Swissair AG as HB-IDK *Matterhorn* on 6 August 1969, this aircraft had been operational with Swissair for 12 years when it was bought by the Perúvian Air Force as FAP370 on 26 December 1981. It was re-registered as OB-1372 in June 1990, leased to Americana de Aviación from March 1993 until October 1993, then withdrawn from use and stored at Jorge Chávez Airport, Lima, in December 1994.

N4934Z Douglas DC-8-63 Hawaiian Airlines at Amsterdam Airport Schiphol, 16 June 1984. It was delivered to Iberia on 2 August 1969 as EC-BQS, then sold to Aviaco on 6 March 1981 and named *Marbelle*. International Air Leases, Inc. bought it as N4934Z on 19 April 1984 and leased it to Hawaiian Airlines from 5 June 1984 until February 1993. The aircraft was withdrawn from use and stored at Kingman Airport in Arizona in February 1993 before being sold to Aerolease Financial Group on 4 February 1994. It was leased to Airborne Express as N822AX, stored and withdrawn from use at Wilmington Air Park, Ohio, and finally scrapped on 8 September 1994.

Left: PH-DEF Douglas DC-8-63 KLM Royal Dutch Airlines *Henry Hudson* at Amsterdam Airport Schiphol, 23 December 1983. Close up!

Below: N728A Douglas DC-8-72 Aramco at Amsterdam Airport Schiphol, June 1986. Originally delivered to United Airlines as a DC-8-62H on 11 August 1969 with registration N8971U, it was leased to Overseas National Airways from 2 July 1973 until 6 August 1973. It returned to United Airlines and was bought by Cammacorp in August 1981 before being was converted to a DC-8-72 with CFM56-2C engines in October 1981. ARAMCO bought it on 22 Janaury 1982 as N728A, then sold it to Aero Turbine in February 2005. It was stored at Opa Locka Airport in Florida and broken up in May 2006. (Peter de Groot)

Above: N817NA Douglas DC-8-72 NASA at Ramstein Air Base, Germany, 24 January 2018. It was first flown on 8 April 1969 and delivered to Alitalia as a DC-8-62H with registration I-DIWK before being sold to Braniff Airways on 7 January 1979 as N801BN. Four years later it was bought by International Air Leases, Inc. in November 1983 and leased to Nacelle Corporation in September 1984. It returned to International Air Leases in December 1985 and was sold to Cammacor which, in turn, sold it to NASA on 4 February 1986. It was converted to a DC-8-72 at Edwards Air Force Base on 21 July 1986 as N717NA, and later re-registered as N817NA. (Peter de Groot)

Below left: N817NA Douglas DC-8-72 NASA (cockpit) at Ramstein Air Base, Germany, 30 January 2018. This DC-8 is based at the NASA Armstrong Flight Research Centre facility in Palmdale, California, and is used to collect data for experiments in support of projects serving the world's scientific community. Federal, state, academic and foreign investigators are among those who use NASA's DC-8-72. In January 2018, there was a NASA project conducted in co-operation with the German air and space industry called 'fuel sniffing', which tested alternative fuel types at different altitudes for future climate protection. The NASA DC-8-72 was based for several weeks at Ramstein Air Base in Germany. There were eight fuel-sniffing flights in total; the fuel sniffing was done at different altitudes and at different speeds in circles over northern Germany, taking approximately six hours per flight. It was quite an experience to fly in the contrails of an Airbus 320 (D-ATRA) to collect its emissions. (Felix Reim)

Below right: Cabin of the NASA DC-8-72 N817NA, Flying Laboratory, with the crew collecting data, flying over northern Germany, 30 January 2018. (Felix Reim)

N817NA Douglas DC-8-72 NASA, flying over northern Germany, looking at the giant CFM56-2C engines, 30 January 2018. (Felix Reim)

N2547R Douglas DC-8-62H Cammacorp Super 70 at Amsterdam Airport Schiphol, June 1983. Originally ordered by United Airlines as a DC-8-62 on 19 August 1969 as N8972U, this aircraft was sold to Air Jamaica on 29 October 1973 as 6Y-JII, and after nine years of service, it was bought by Cammacorp on 1 December 1982 as N2547R and converted to a DC-8-72 with CFM56-2C5 engines in January 1983. It was sold to Bright Star Enterprises in August 1984, then sold again in March 1987 to the Saudi Arabian government as HZ-MS11. Re-registered as HZ-HM11 in 1993, it was later flown to Dallas Love Field in Texas and stored in October 1995. The aircraft was bought by TriStar International Sales, Inc. on 14 October 1996 and broken up during December 2003. In April 1984, Cammacorp made one major improvement to the DC-8: an FAA (Federal Aviation Administration) supplemental type certificate was awarded for a glass cockpit version of the DC-8-72. (Peter de Groot)

N4866T Douglas DC-8-73CF Transamerica Airlines at Amsterdam Airport Schiphol, 5 March 1983. It was delivered to TIA on 29 December 1969 as N4866T, leased to Aeronaves de Mexico from March 1971 until March 1974 and returned to TIA. The airline was renamed as Transamerica on 1 October 1979 and the aircraft leased to Air Afrique and Spirit of America Airlines. It was bought by GPA Group in February 1987, which leased it to Flying Tiger Line as N707FT in June 1988. It was re-registered to N407FE after the merge with Fedex Express in August 1989. It was sold to UPS in July 1990 as N811UP and stored at Roswell Airport on 26 February 2009 before being scrapped during 2011.

N873SJ Douglas DC-8-73CF Southern Air Transport at Ostend Airport, 8 June 1997. Delivered to TIA on 15 April 1970 as N4868T, it has a long history of owners and lease companies, including Transamerica, Minerve France, Southern Air Transport, AeroUsa, Challenge Air, DHL, Emery Worldwide, and Astar Air Cargo as N873SJ from 30 June 2003 until 10 April 2013. It went to Skybus Jet Cargo and then Perúvian Airlines as OB-2158-P on 22 April 2018, returning to Skybus Jet Cargo on 31 March 2021.

OB-2158-P Douglas DC-8-73CF Skybus Jet Cargo arriving at San José Airport in Costa Rica, 4 February 2022. Skybus Jet Cargo is a Perúvian Cargo Airline and the only airline in the world still operating two civilian DC-8-73s. The first DC-8-73, OB-2059-P, was bought in November 2016, and the second, OB-2158-P, in March 2021. The airline's main office is in Lima, Perú, and it flies mainly to Panama, Costa Rica, Colombia, Barbados and Paramaribo in Suriname. During a flight from Medellín Airport in Colombia to Miami on 21 January 2018, the DC-8-73 experienced a very long take-off roll at Medellín Airport. The aircraft became airborne just short of the end of Runway 01 and climbed away safely. Runway 01 is 3,700m long. It is still active as of May 2022. (Jose Salazar)

PH-DEG Douglas DC-8-63 KLM Royal Dutch Airlines at Panama City Tocumen Airport, 20 November 1971. KLM ground staff are waiting at the ramp for the arrival of the DC-8. This was our flight to Amsterdam from Panama via Curaçao, Caracas, Madrid and Zürich, with a flying time of 17 hours, 2 minutes. Delivered to KLM on 23 December 1969, after 14 years of service it was bought by Capitol Air on 26 November 1984 as N926CL. It was used by several airlines, such as Emery Air Freight, Airlift International, and National Airlines as N951R on September 1985. It was damaged on 20 August 1987 at Newburgh Stewart Airport: it clipped the tail section of a Douglas DC-9 that was vacating the runway after landing. The DC-8's port side engine was ripped off the wing in the collision, but there were no casualties. It was withdrawn from use on 13 August 2001 (location unknown).

ZS-OSI Douglas DC-8-62H African International at Istanbul Sabiha Gökçen Airport, 27 March 2006. It was delivered to Alitalia as I-DIWW on 10 February 1970, and stored at Marana Airport in April 1981, Sea & Sun Airlines bought it on March 1983 as N39305 and then sold it to MGM Grand Air in January 1988. It was converted to a DC-8-62(F) freighter in June 1995 as N802MG for American International Airways and later went to Champion Air, Kitty Hawk, and African International Airways in January 2002 as 3D-AIA. The aircraft was re-registered as ZS-OSI in March 2002, stored in November 2012 and broken up at Manston Airport, UK, in February 2015.

N917R Douglas DC-8-71 Icelandair at Luxemburg Airport, 19 April 1985. It was delivered to Japan Airlines as a DC-8-61 JA8041 on 15 January 1970, bought by Overseas National in June 1981 as N917R and leased to Saudi and Icelandair between 1981 and 1983. It was converted to a DC-8-71 with CFM56-2C engines and flown by many airlines, including National Airlines, Point Air, Kenya Airways, and Zambia Airways as 9J-AFL in October 1989. The aircraft was sold to Aerolease on 11 March 1995 and converted to a DC-8-71(F) freighter and leased to Emery Worldwide as N811AL in October 1995. It was was withdrawn from use on 13 August 2001 and broken up at Roswell Airport, New Mexico, in 2005.

N8630 Douglas DC-8-63CF Air Bahama at Brussels Zaventem Airport, 25 July 1972. It was delivered to Seaboard World Airlines on 25 September 1969 as N8630 and leased to International Air Bahama on 21 May 1970. The airline was renamed Air Bahama in June 1972 and the aircraft was bought by Icelandair in November 1977 as TF-FLE, operating for Air Bahama. It was leased to ONA and National Airlines before Orion Air bought it on 1 August 1984. The DC-8-63CF was converted to a DC-8-73CF with CFM56-2C engines and transferred to United Parcel Service in 1988. It was withdrawn from use and stored at Roswell Airport, New Mexico, in 2009.

OB-1260 Douglas DC-8-62 AeroPerú at Mexico City International Airport, 28 October 1989. It was ordered by SAS and delivered on 30 January 1970 as LN-MOG. Leased to Swissair from October 1971 until November 1980, it was then sold to AeroPerú on 3 December 1982 as OB-R1260. The aircraft was re-registered as OB-1260 in September 1989 and stored at Lima Jorge Chávez Airport in August 1990.

N796FT Douglas DC-8-73CF Emery Worldwide Airlines at Amsterdam Airport Schiphol, 23 August 1993. It was delivered to Flying Tiger Line as a DC-8-63CF on 3 October 1969 as N797FT, leased to Air India from 16 August 1981 until November 1982 and returned to Flying Tiger before being sold to Connecticut National Bank in May 1984. It was leased to Emery Worldwide (renamed Emery Worldwide Airlines in 1991) in May 1984 and converted to a DC-8-73CF. The aircraft was sold to Aerofreighter on 25 November 2002 and stored at Pinal Airpark in Arizona on 4 January 2001. It was bought by BETA Cargo as PP-BEX in October 2004, withdrawn from use and stored at Lima Jorge Chávez Airport during 2009.

EC-892 Douglas DC-8-62 Canarias Cargo at Miami International Airport, 8 May 1995. Originally delivered to Braniff Airways on 23 October 1969 as N1808E, it was bought by International Air Leases in June 1983 and leased to Rich International Airways in October 1983. The aircraft was converted to a DC-8-62(F) in November 1990 and leased to Arrow Air on 15 December 1990, followed by another lease to Canarias Cargo on 8 May 1995 as EC-892. It was re-registered as EC-GCY on 4 August 1995 and returned to International Air Leases on 27 April 1996 as N1808E. Arrow Air leased it on 11 October 1996, and it was bought by Agro Air on 10 March 1999. On the night of 28 April 2002, the DC-8-62(F) arrived at Changi International Airport in Singapore. While taxiing, the aircraft came to a halt when its main landing gears went into a drainage ditch. It sustained substantial damage and was written off.

N1809E Douglas DC-8-62 *Fajalobi* Surinam Airways at Paramaribo Zanderij Airport, Suriname, 28 May 1986. It was first flown on 3 October 1969 and delivered to Braniff Airways as N1809E on 17 November 1969. Bought by International Air Leases on 15 June 1983, it was leased to Arrow Air on 21 December 1983 and sub-leased to Surinam Airways on 6 January 1984, Surinam Airways bought the aircraft in March 1986 and leased it to Tropical Airways from 10 July 1987 until 2 August 1987. Surinam Airways flight PY764 from Amsterdam Schiphol Airport to Paramaribo Zanderij International Airport, on 7 June 1989, crashed on its approach as a result of the captain's glaring carelessness and recklessness: he flew below the published minimum altitude during the approach. Consequently, its No. 2 engine collided with a tree; the right wing then struck another tree, causing the aircraft to roll, striking the ground inverted. The aircraft broke up and caught on fire. There were no survivors.

9S-AJG Douglas DC-8-62(F) Trans Air Cargo Service at Johannesburg O R Tombo International Airport, 9 April 2021. Trans Air Cargo Service was started by Jacques 'Kiki' Lemaire in 1992 as Transair Cargo, but it shut down in 1998 due to the civil war in Congo. Transair Congo was renamed TAC Air Service and moved to Johannesburg Rand Airport in June 1998. It restarted again in the Democratic Republic of the Congo in late 2004 after a rename to Trans Air Cargo Service, with Max Lemaire as the general director for the cargo carrier based out of Kinshasa N'Djili International Airport. Delivered to United Airlines on 23 September 1969 as N8974U, this aircraft has seen service with a variety of airlines, including Arrow Air, ATI, LAP Paraguay, Rich International, African International Airways, and it was delivered to Trans Air Cargo Service in July 2007 as 9S-CJG, re-registered as 9S-AJG. As of 23 April 2022, it is still flying daily from Kinshasa to Lubumbashi, Goma and Kisangani. (Timothy Connor Brandt)

N866F Douglas DC-8-63CF ONA at Nice Côte d`Azur Airport, 10 May 1978. It was delivered to United Airlines as N8774U on 23 September 1969 and has a long list of operators: Seaboard World Airlines, Cargolux, Loftleider, Saudi, Nigeria Airways, Flying Tiger Line, Icelandair and Air India. It was bought by UPS on 30 September 1984 as N776FT and re-registered as N812UP in January 1985. The aircraft was withdrawn from use and stored at Roswell, New Mexico, in 2009, and bought by AerSale, Inc. in 2010.

9G-AXA Douglas DC-8-63(F) Air Charter Express take-off shot at Ostend Airport, Bruges, 26 July 2008. Originally delivered to Air Canada on 12 March 1970 as CF-TIU, it was withdrawn from use and stored at Marana Airport in Arizona in May 1983. The aircraft was converted to a DC-8-63(F) in February 1986, bought by Evergreen International Airlines as N818EV on 30 October 1988 and sold to Airborne Express on 2 March 1990 as N811AX. It was later bought by Air Charter Express as 9G-AXA in March 2007 and two years later it was sold to Meridian Airways in September 2009 as 9G-AXA. It was stored at Ostend Airport in 2010 and returned to service on 15 September 2011 and has been seen stored at Yaounde Nsimalen International Airport in Cameroon. (Kristof Jonckheere)

ZP-CCH Douglas DC-8-63 Líneas Aéreas Paraguayas at Asunción Airport, Paraguay. This was my flight from Asunción to Brussels via Dakar and Madrid on 19 November 1988. Delivered to Air Canada as CF-TIX on 23 May 1970, this aircraft was re-registered as C-FTIX in April 1983. It was withdrawn from use at Dorval Airport, Montreal, during 1983 and was bought by LAP on 20 December 1984. It was stored at Asunción Airport from March 1994 until January 1995 and then sold to Airborne Express on 25 January 1995 as N825AX, being scrapped on 25 April 2007 (location unknown).

ZP-CCH Douglas DC-8-63 LAP. Cockpit shot flying from Brussels Airport to Asunción in Paraguay via Tenerife. On the left is Comandante Insaurralde, next to his co-pilot, Cespedes. (Michel Anciaux)

PH-DEK Douglas DC-8-63 KLM with an old white top colour scheme at Amsterdam Airport Schiphol, 24 May 1971. It was ordered by Philippine Airlines but not taken up, and instead delivered to KLM Royal Dutch Airlines as PH-DEK *David Livingstone* on 25 November 1969. It was leased to Philippine Airlines from 1 May 1972 until 1 May 1975 before returning to KLM and being sold to Icelandair on 5 November 1984 as TF-FLV. It was bought by Aer Turas as EI-CAK on 31 May 1990 and converted to a DC-8-63(F) in September 1990. After four years of service, Aer Turas sold the aircraft to Aerolease Finance Corp as N786AL on 13 June 1994. It was then leased to ATI on 26 September 1994 and bought by Race Aviation on 2 June 2004. Its registration was cancelled, and it was exported to Ghana as 9G-FAB for Johnson Air in July 2004. The aircraft was stored at Ras Al Khaimah International Airport, UAE, and broken up in 2010.

PH-DEL Douglas DC-8-63 African Safari Airways at Amsterdam Airport Schiphol, 24 March 1982. It was ordered by Philippine Airlines but not taken up and instead bought by KLM, delivered on 31 December 1969 as PH-DEL. It was leased to Philippine Airlines from 1 April 1973 until 1 May 1975 and, after returning to KLM, was leased to African Safari Airways on 24 March 1982 before being bought on 6 June 1982 as 5Y-ZEB. It was sold to Airborne Express on 19 January 1994 as N823AX, stored at Wilmington Airpark, Ohio, on 7 March 2006 and broken up for spares.

PH-DEL Douglas DC-8-63 Philippine Airlines at Amsterdam Airport Schiphol, 28 March 1973. In its pursuit of a worldwide network of services, KLM has been eyeing up Philippine Airlines (PAL) for some time. In March 1962, KLM and Philippine Airlines signed a multi-year co-operation agreement, which covered subjects ranging from co-ordination of timetables and marketing to training of PAL personnel by KLM and technical integration of the aircraft equipment. To enable PAL to build up an international route network with modern equipment, KLM made one of its DC-8 aircraft available to PAL, and later also supplied it with Douglas DC-10s.

N801WA Douglas DC-8-63CF World Airways at Amsterdam Schiphol Airport, 21 April 1972. Although ordered by Airlift International, it was not taken up and bought by World Airways, being delivered on 19 March 1971 as N801WA. The aircraft was leased to many airlines, including Icelandair, ONA, Capitol Air, VIASA, National, Rosenbalm, and Cygnus Air as EC-IGZ in July 2002. It had already been converted to a DC-8-73CF freighter with CFM56-2C engines. It was bought by Trans Air Cargo Service as 3X-GHH on 25 November 2011 and then re-registered as 9S-AJO for Trans Air Cargo Service in 2019. It was still active last year flying from Kinshasa to Goma in the Democratic Republic of the Congo.

9Q-CJO Douglas DC-8-73CF Trans Air Cargo Service at Kinshasa N'Djili International Airport, 2 June 2016. Ex-Cygnus Air EC-IGZ was withdrawn from use in December 2009 at Madrid-Barajas Airport and sold to Trans Air Cargo Service (TACS) as 3X-GHH on 25 November 2011. It was re-registered as 9Q-CJO first and later as 9S-AJO in 2019. At time of writing (April 2022), the DC-8-73CF is at Kinshasa N'Djili International Airport for a C-check at the Trans Air Cargo maintenance area. (Congo – Zaïre Aviation)

TU-TCF Douglas DC-8-63CF Air Afrique *Fort Lamy* at Paris Le Bourget Airport, 16 January 1972. It was delivered to Air Afrique on 28 May 1970 as TU-TCF and bought by Aerolease Financial Group as N784AL on 17 December 1991. It was leased to several airlines, including Arrow Air, Airtransport International, American International Airways and BAX Global. It was also leased to Aerofreighter from January 1999 until March 2001, and then to Arrow Air again from 30 September 2002 until 22 March 2004. The aircraft was withdrawn from use in 2009 and scrapped at an unknown location.

PH-DEM Douglas DC-8-63 Surinam Airways at Amsterdam Airport Schiphol, 23 September 1979. It was the 11th order by KLM and the last of the 63 series ordered by KLM. Delivered on 22 June 1970 as PH-DEM, it was leased to Surinam Airways from 3 November 1975 until October 1983. After returning to KLM, it was sold to Seychelles International as S7-SIS on 10 December 1983 and was re-registered as HB-IBF for African Safari Airways on 1 December 1987. The aircraft was bought by ABX Air on 27 January 1994 as N824AX, stored and withdrawn from use at Wilmington Airpark, Ohio, in June 2002.

PH-DEM Douglas DC-8-63 Surinam Airways at Amsterdam Airport Schiphol, 24 October 1982. KLM maintenance area.

OB-R-1210 Douglas DC-8-62H AeroPerú at Rio de Janeiro Galeao Airport, 23 October 1988. It was delivered to Alitalia on 12 March 1971 as I-DIWX and bought by AeroPerú on 19 February 1981 as OB-R-1210. It was re-registered as OB-1210 in November 1989, stored at Lima's Jorge Chávez Airport in August 1993 and bought by GMD, Inc. as N61CX in January 1994. The aircraft was converted to a DC-8-62(F) and leased to ATI on 21 November 1994, then sub-leased to Kuwait Airways from October 1997 until July 1998. After returning to ATI, it was bought by Aerofreighter in December 1999 and stored at Pinal Airpark, Arizona.

C-GQBA Douglas DC-8-63 Quebecair at Manchester Airport, September 1985. Delivered to Iberia on 23 December 1970 as EC-BSE, this aircraft was bought by International Air Leases as N940JW in November 1983 and leased to Arrow Air. It returned to International Air Leases in May 1984 and was leased to Quebecair from 3 May 1984 until September 1986 as C-GQBA. It was finally sold to ABX Air on 18 January 1992 as N820AX and stored and withdrawn from use at Wilmington Airport, Ohio, on 15 May 2007.

EC-BSE Douglas DC-8-63 Iberia at La Paz El Alto Airport, Bolivia, 17 December 1974. This was my flight from La Paz to Lima in Perú. La Paz El Alto Airport sits at an altitude of 13,325ft (4,061m); it is the highest international airport and the sixth highest commercial airport in the world (the highest commercial airport outside of China). Its runway is 13,123ft (4,000m)

N810ZA Douglas DC-8-62AF Zantop International at Amsterdam Airport Schiphol, 12 June 1987. First flown on 21 February 1972 and ordered by Japan Airlines as JA8056, it was delivered on 21 March 1972. Zantop International Airlines bought it on 20 August 1984 as N810ZA before selling it to CF Air Freight on 1 August 1988. The aircraft was re-registered as N996F in July 1989 and sold to Air Trading International in May 2002. United Arabian Airlines bought it in March 2004 as ST-UAA and sold it on to Gabon Cargo as TR-LIC in December 2006. Avient Air Zimbabwe was the next buyer in August 2008 (as Z-ALB) followed by a quick sale to Air Charter Express as 9G-AED in December 2008. It was withdrawn from use at Cape Town Airport in November 2012 for Star Away Aviation as ZS-YDB.

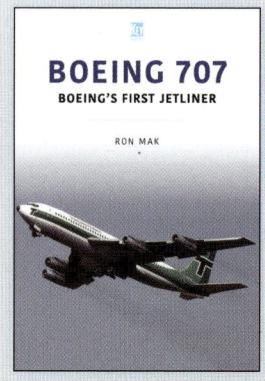
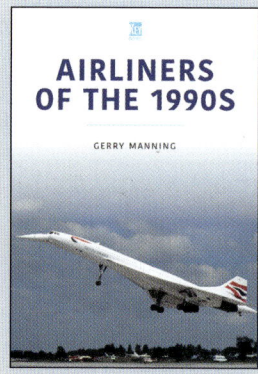
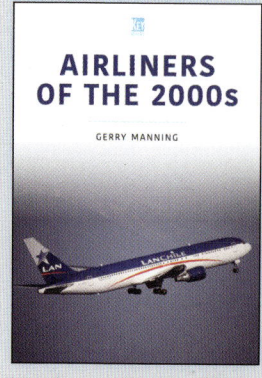

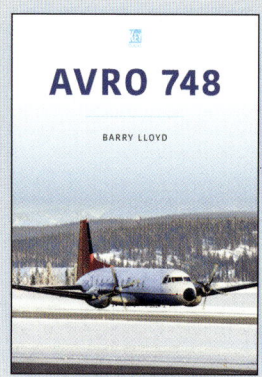
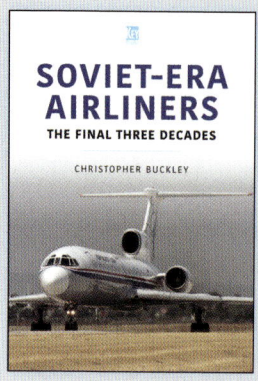